A GUIDE TO
Creating
Student-Staffed
Writing Centers

GRADES 6–12

PETER LANG
New York • Washington, D.C./Baltimore • Bern
Frankfurt am Main • Berlin • Brussels • Vienna • Oxford

RICHARD KENT

A GUIDE TO
Creating
Student-Staffed
Writing Centers

GRADES 6–12

PETER LANG
New York • Washington, D.C./Baltimore • Bern
Frankfurt am Main • Berlin • Brussels • Vienna • Oxford

Library of Congress Cataloging-in-Publication Data
Kent, Richard.
A guide to creating student-staffed writing centers,
grades 6–12 / Richard Kent.
p. cm.
Includes bibliographical references and index.
1. English language—Composition and exercises—Study and teaching
(Middle school). 2. English language—Composition and exercises—
Study and teaching (Secondary). 3. Writing centers.
4. Peer-group tutoring of students. I. Title.
LB1631.K455   808'.042'0712—dc22   2005012815
ISBN 978-0-8204-7889-0

Bibliographic information published by **Die Deutsche Bibliothek**.
Die Deutsche Bibliothek lists this publication in the "Deutsche
Nationalbibliografie"; detailed bibliographic data is available
on the Internet at http://dnb.ddb.de/.

Cover design by Lisa Barfield

The paper in this book meets the guidelines for permanence and durability
of the Committee on Production Guidelines for Book Longevity
of the Council of Library Resources.

© 2006, 2010 Peter Lang Publishing, Inc., New York
29 Broadway, 18th floor, New York, NY 10006
www.peterlang.com

Printed in the United States of America

For my brother, Rob,
who gave me my
first real writing machine—
an IBM, of course.

Contents

Acknowledgments

T he first writing center staff at Mountain Valley High School in Rumford, Maine, taught me about the possibilities of student-staffed writing centers and the promise of the secondary English classroom. *Your Loving English Teacher* thanks Amy Law Goodwin, Amy Welch, Craig Dickson, Chris Larsen, Dave Kasregis, Erin Adams Gurney, Jamie Ippolito, Janet Hoyle, Kathy MacDougall Oldakowski, Matt Irish, Matt Gaudet, Mike Gawtry, and Scott Marchildon.

I am indebted to Dave Boardman, Judy Hogan and Joanne Sobolik, and Peggy Silva for sharing their stories and welcoming me into their secondary school writing centers in person and via phone, email, and Internet. Pam Childers, Dawn Fels, and Lee Ann Spillane generously shared their knowledge, materials, and writing center work. Many members of the writing center community across America answered email queries and fielded phone calls. Some of those generous folks include Neal Lerner and Paula Gillespie, John Duffy and Connie Mack, Gayla Keesee and Carole D. Overton, Muriel "Mickey" Harris, Ben Rafoth, Roberta Kjesrud, Barclay Barrios, Jon Olson, Josh Gould, Jeanette Jordan, Clint Gardner, and my new friend, Harvey Kail.

My sincere appreciation to Ryan Middleswart, a future English-teaching, soccer-coaching star, for his thoughtful feedback and research; Michal Cicala, my Slovakian computer guide; my former principal, Tom Rowe, whose "Go for it!" started the adventure; the International Association of Writing Centers; Maureen Montgomery, for indexing and lunchtime conversations; participants in the Secondary School Writing Centers List; participants in the Writing Center Mailing List digest; Carol Ellis, for modeling what writing center directors can be; and my UMaine and Maine Writing Project colleagues for their friendship and teachings.

Bernadette Shade, my production supervisor at Peter Lang Publishing, answered my many questions with kindness and expertise. Chris Myers, my Peter Lang editor and fellow Mainer, offered thoughtful advice. And as always, Anne Wood, editor *extraordinaire*, guided with insight and wit.

CHAPTER ONE

Introduction

A Day in the Life of a Writing Center

It's 7:30 in the morning and two bleary-eyed 9th grade girls peek around the doorframe. Tabitha, the writing center student on duty, smiles. She figures the girls are from Mr. St. John's class—all of his students are writing multi-genre papers this month and must bring the papers in for a conference. At 7:38, Jeff and Lindy arrive to help with two more of Mr. St. John's students.

Housed in the media center/library, the writing center creates lots of extra traffic, but Mr. Sassi, the media center specialist, loves the comings and goings. Most of all, he enjoys sneaking glimpses of kids working with kids.

During first period, Dustin swaggers in. The first draft of his reading autobiography is due on Friday—it's Wednesday. "I don't have a clue what to write," he moans.

To get to know him, Marcy chats a bit with Dustin. Finally, she suggests, "Let's make a list of things that you've read in your life." She helps him create a list, including snowboard magazines, comics, and a weekly magazine that has ads to sell everything; he's also reminded of the picture books his mom read to him when he was younger. In fifteen minutes Dustin is on his way with a blueprint for the paper.

During 3rd period, three senior writing center staffers go to Mrs. Tyler's class to confer with students during their writing workshop time. Mark staffs the writing center by himself, and except for a steady stream of kids coming in to use the computers, no one needs his help in the first hour. During the last thirty minutes of the period, he talks to three A.P. Biology students who are writing a brochure on Lyme disease for a group project.

At lunchtime fourteen students work at the computers while three student-editors, all seniors, sit around the main desk cramming for a physics test. A wiry boy fingering a paper peers in, sees the seniors, and bolts. "I'll go get him," says Jason, pushing aside his physics notes. Jason returns with the boy and spends ten minutes discussing the tenth-grader's paper with him.

When the dismissal bell sounds at 2:25 pm, fifty-three kids make a beeline for the lecture hall. A fifteen-minute S.A.T. study session called "Slaying the

Dragon" is being offered. Today, it's sentence completions.. By 3:00 in the afternoon when Ian tallies the writing center's logbook, twenty-eight students have visited the center for conferences and seventy-seven have used the computers. The twenty-three kids in Mrs. Tyler's 3rd period class and the S.A.T. crew are counted on separate tally sheets.

The writing center is closed for the day.

Where Writers Work with Writers

Writing centers, writing labs, writing workshops, or writers' centers are places where writers talk with fellow writers about their work in an effort to discover a thesis, overcome procrastination, develop ideas, create an outline, evaluate a draft, or revise a draft. Writing center staff members support, tutor, and confer with writers in an effort to encourage and motivate. In the most effective writing centers, student writers feel at ease as they create and revise lab reports, applications, essays, projects, digital stories, poems, cover letters, iMovies, resumes, short stories, songs, research papers, personal letters, etc.

Many of us who direct writing centers take on the position in lieu of another duty, for a reduced class load, or as a volunteer. A few middle and high school centers have full-time faculty-directors; however, this isn't common. Most colleges, universities, and community colleges in the United States have writing centers, but few middle or high schools do. Since there are writing centers in post-secondary schools, this fact may be the largest selling point in creating one at your school. And there are many other reasons, too.

Why Writing Centers?

I could not be the primary editor for my many student writers if I wanted them to produce a good deal of revised writing during the course of the school year.
                                                                    —Richard Kent (1997, 50)

During the first year of my English teaching life, I carried stacks of papers home to "correct," just as my own high school English teachers had. For hour upon hour, I penciled marginal notations and comma corrections. I drew long squiggly lines across the pages in an attempt to guide my young writers in reorganizing sentences, paragraphs, or entire papers. We English teachers know the drill.

It didn't take long for me to realize a couple of truths about my technique: First, my single edit of 100–120 student papers, usually without an extended consultation, didn't parallel how my own editor worked with me as a writer. She didn't try to "correct" a piece; she conferred with me draft after draft after draft. She respected the process and nurtured mine without rushing.

With my students' papers, I tried to do it all in one fell swoop. Because of the number of students I worked with, and because I could not conceive of another way, I had an assembly-line approach and bled on their papers. As I look back now, I see that I mangled papers, left students confused, and ignored process. Even worse, I probably discouraged some student writers.

For my talented and self-assured writers—perhaps ten percent of my kids—these corrections were viewed as a fun challenge. These students knew how to play the game and translate what Mr. Kent "suggested" into the "A" they wanted and usually received. My wild rants on the paper made them smile—they showed these mutilated papers to their friends as a kind of badge of honor.

However, for most of my students, those who lacked confidence in their writing and in so many other areas of their lives, my editorial carnage confounded and discouraged. As a result of my corrections these students "fixed" lower-order technique issues such as comma errors and misspellings, but when it came to real revision, it didn't happen in profound ways. How do I know? All I had to do was compare drafts side by side: the second-draft papers were cleaner and more technically correct, but as for focus and development, those higher-order writing issues, not much changed. In fact, for these kids my editorial scribbles probably made writing more mysterious and more difficult, if not plain misery.

And thus the second truth: I could not be the primary editor for my many student writers if I wanted them to produce a good deal of revised writing during the course of the school year. Clearly, I needed help.

Prior to high school teaching, I taught College Writing 100 at a university not far from my home. For three and a half years, I taught three to four sections per semester and required all of my students to use the university's writing center. To be honest, I didn't know anything about writing centers at the time. My university supervisor directed the writing center, and he asked me to add a writing center consultation into my students' writing process. Naturally, sending my students to his center seemed like a fine idea—and it was.

Near the end of my first year of teaching high school, I thought about that university writing center and the benefits the conferences provided my college writing students. The writing center tutors carried on the essential conversations; they helped students develop, organize, and express their ideas more clearly. The tutors were a godsend because they engaged my students in longer conversations about their writing—conversations I could not sustain because of time constraints. Yes, we workshopped in our class, but these first-year college students needed more. So did my high school kids.

In the spring of my first year of teaching, I visited a high school writing center in the southern part of the state. I liked what I saw and knew that both my students and I needed this kind of support. I invited two students from my junior English classes to serve as student-directors that next year, and we started to organize. I read *The High School Writing Center: Establishing and Maintaining One* (1989) edited by Pamela Farrell and published by the National Council of Teachers of English. For those of us creating secondary writing centers in the 1990s, this book explored issues, answered questions, and made our work seem possible. Pam Childers (formerly Farrell) has been a steady central voice in the secondary school writing center world.

The Mountain Valley Writing Center went through many changes over a ten-year period in our small-town high school of 525 students. When I moved on to work toward my final academic degree, the writing center closed. Several administrative changes—not uncommon at our school (I worked with eight principals in ten years)—a first-year teacher replacement, and no willing person to take on the volunteer directorship, let the writing center slip away. Presently, two MVHS English teachers have been speaking with me about a writing center resurrection!

During our first year, twelve students worked out of the back of my English classroom. A supportive principal convinced the superintendent and school board to reduce my teaching load by two sections; the assistant director had hers reduced by one class. At the time, our high school operated on a traditional seven-period day. The writing center's twelve student-editors and the two faculty-directors staffed the writing center during thirty class periods a week. About one third of the faculty sent students to the center, and by the end of the year over 2,000 clients had visited, including students, teachers, administrators, two secretaries, a custodian, a school board member, and the superintendent of schools.

Our handpicked group of writing center staff represented a cross-section of the student body. However, these young people had one common trait: Other kids liked them. In addition, these student-editors, most of whom planned to attend college, enjoyed writing or realized why writing was important to their futures. Recognizing the need to show the maximum potential of a writing center, I selected these specific students in an effort to help the writing center gain status. Clearly, I was a political animal. During the founding year, 1990–1991, our school had only one computer lab. As a result, the four writing center computers—something akin to Apple II gs with one

Apple Imagewriter printer—also served as enticements. The daisy-wheel printer and an endless supply of paper didn't hurt either.

We didn't open for business that first year until mid-September. I spent the first few weeks working with our twelve editors. During that abbreviated quarter, we worked with 496 clients. The second year of operation eighteen student-editors signed up for a writing center English class, and by year three the staff numbered thirty-seven. The center opened thirty minutes before school began and closed thirty minutes after—at 7:30 a.m. and 3:00 p.m. We had our own room with twenty computers and two large desks for tutors and their clients. Amazingly, during our third year no faculty or adult staff members were on duty in the writing center during the day. A faculty colleague in the social studies department "supervised" from just across the hallway. He would pop in periodically, and I visited the center when time permitted. This student-supervised writing center lasted one year. A sixteen-year old knuckle-dragger threw a three-ring binder and a dictionary out the window in late May and that was the end of that. The next year teachers were assigned to the writing center as one of their duties. During my last three years at the high school, the writing center thrived in the media center/library, thanks to our gracious librarian. At this time we were up to about sixty writing center staff members.

What the Writing Center Did for the Student Staffers

Those kids who staffed The Writing Center gained confidence, perspective, and understanding as writers and as people. During the school week, and sometimes over weekends, these young writers would confer with a variety of clients, including would-be Ivy Leaguers wanting one more response to college entrance essays and fifteen-year-old kids with learning differences who struggled to compose a single paragraph. Our writing tutors learned through experience how to listen carefully and respect the writing and thinking process. Most student-editors grew to understand how important it was to highlight and compliment a client's strong passages as a way to motivate and to help writers identify their own strengths. These editors also came to recognize that making suggestions for revision was a subtle art form: "You might like to think about" or "I wonder if this...." These students showed care for both author and text.

Our novice editors, typically less secure with their own writing than more seasoned editors, swaggered through students' essays, bleeding high and low. These students ignored the process and corrected not unlike what I had done as an English teacher "BWC" (before the writing center). I could pick out these student-editors by watching from the other side of the room. There was little or no conversation between editor and writer: the editor often took the text away from the writer to bleed slashes, arrows, and scribbles across the pages. These novice editors thought little about the story being told or, worse yet, the storyteller: their main concern was correctness. We know as editors that correcting a comma splice or a misspelling is much easier and much less time-consuming than listening to the story of a story. We know that helping a writer develop a character more fully or revise passive constructions takes revision after revision. There are no short cuts through the process.

In time, by working with clients and through conversations in the writing center English class, our student-editors began to understand how effective editors work with writers. I continually reminded them to recall how unnerving it was to hand over a piece of writing. These students grew to value the power of listening, the necessity of encouragement, and the respect of process. Editing sessions began with personal conversations beyond the writing assignment and often ended with "Let me see what you come up with in the next couple of days."

What the Writing Center Did for Me as a Teacher

After the center was up and running, I rarely took papers home at night to "correct." My role changed from corrector to writing coach. I conferred with my student writers throughout the school day, but I didn't have to attempt to carry on individual conversations about individual papers with up to 120 individual student writers. When I tried to be everyone's editor, our conversations in class were superficial and quick. I'm also convinced that my input, especially written comments and corrections throughout their papers, rarely moved student writers toward genuine revision. With me as their primary editor, my students were revising papers only once or twice. In addition, as the authority in the class (i.e., the adult with the college degree who assigned grades), when I "suggested" a change to a paper, the student made the change. Very few students questioned my suggestions; they simply corrected whatever I pointed out because I held the key to their success. That's just not how writers and their editors should work.

(If you're interested in this power dynamic, read works about power and authority in schools and the classroom from critical pedagogues such as Paulo Freire, Peter McLaren, Michel Foucault, and Antonia Darder. Also read works by composition theorists such as Peter Elbow and Donald Murray.)

My English teaching life changed forever as a result of the writing center and the establishment of a portfolio-based classroom (Kent, 1997; Kent, 2000). My students produced four portfolios a year, one every 8–9 weeks, each portfolio typically containing the following:

- Three highly-revised papers, usually 3–5 drafts, about 1000 words long (I asked students to attach all drafts and to have their editors sign and date the drafts)
- Two papers, revised once, about 1000 words long (again, their editors signed and dated the drafts)
- Forty-eight, one-page journal entries, first draft, spell-checked only (if word processed), about 150 words in length
- Five books read (self-selected)
- Three to five book projects created and presented
- One written reflection of the class, themselves as students, their portfolios, and me about 1000 words

The availability of student-editors offered in-school support, and ninety-minute block periods gave even more significant workshop time. Both the writing center staff and the institution's time frame supported my English students in producing a good deal of writing.

A writing center may not help you reinvent your teaching as it did for me, but with a writing center you won't feel as alone and the conversations among writers will be enriched. Ultimately, your students' writing will improve because (1) they are writing a lot and (2) they are talking a lot about that writing with someone that they have asked to help them.

What the Writing Center Did for Our School

I'm remembering when my principal said, "Just having 'The Writing Center' sign hanging in the corridor puts a new focus on writing in our school" (see Photo 1-1, Lindy and Jeff Staffing The Writing Center). Conversations among students and staff blossomed as we began promoting the writing center. I wrote an introductory letter to the school staff titled "Eight Ways to Use The Writing Center" (see Figure 1-1) and the student-editors talked it up with their teachers and friends. We composed and printed writing center brochures, bookmarks, and hallway passes. I'll share different promotional materials later on in the book. We worked to address issues of writing across the curriculum, too (see Figure 1-2).

Photo 1-1. Lindy and Jeff Staffing The Writing Center

The Writing Center @ Mountain Valley High School

TO: Staff Colleagues
FR: Rich Kent, The Writing Center
RE: Eight Ways to Use The Writing Center
DT: Thursday, October 4, 1990

In its first week of operation, The Writing Center welcomed seventy-eight clients—in the second week we worked with about 100 students and staff members. The average visit lasted twenty-five minutes. We are busy, but we can do more! Here are Eight Ways to Use Our School's Writing Center:

1. Assign a piece of writing and make it a requirement to have one of the drafts reviewed with a member of The Writing Center staff. Such a

visit takes a short amount of time, but it will emphasize your commitment to quality written work.

2. Assign a short piece of writing (e.g., journal entry) and require your students to word process the first draft in The Writing Center. This assignment will insure that they are creating on a computer and that they have visited The Writing Center.

3. Encourage your students to attend "Slaying the Dragon," our SAT Seminar. Usually, such workshops cost a lot of money: Ours is Free!

4. Encourage your senior students to come in to look at model resumes and to create one of their own.

5. Encourage those students applying to college to have their college entrance essays reviewed in The Writing Center.

6. Bring your own written work (e.g., curricula vitae, syllabi) into The Writing Center for a review.

7. Volunteer as an editor in The Writing Center—it will improve your writing and sharpen your eye.

8. Sign up three to five students per class to come to The Writing Center for conferences on their writing or to use the computers.

Figure 1-1, Eight Ways to Use The Writing Center

The Writing Center
@ Mountain Valley High School

TO: Math Department Friends
FR: Rich Kent, The Writing Center
RE: Writing & Math
DT: October 9, 1990

The attached article, "Writing Letters to Learn Math" by Bill Kennedy (*Learning*, February 1985, pp. 59-61) opens an interesting avenue to writing and mathematics. I thought you'd enjoy this short article especially since we have guests coming in a few weeks from the University of Maine at Farmington to speak about writing across the curriculum. I really liked Kennedy's idea about keeping math journals.

Figure 1-2, Writing Across the Curriculum Memo

A ripple of writing talk turned into a swell and rolled through the school in small and large ways. I heard about journals in math class, revision talk on science research papers, and creative writing in history classes. In a few years, portfolios emerged in eight or more teachers' classrooms, including health, English, science, and social studies. The presence of a writing center created new awareness. Conversation about writing increased and so did writing across the curriculum.

Theoretical Foundation for Writing Centers

Writing is not a solitary act. Writers work with editors and other writers; they think about their readers and after the act of writing and publishing, writers react to their readers' responses. Writers think and listen as readers, writers, and participants in the world. When I write an article on playing soccer, I write as soccer player, soccer coach, writer, academic, and editor. I share my work with my personal editor and with the publication's editor and perhaps its editorial board. It's not uncommon for me to share a draft of my article with several soccer players of different ages and with coaching colleagues. Yes, I spend a good deal of time alone at the computer in that recursive slow dance that is writing, but the rest of my time is social, conversational, very much a community affair. That's how writers work.

The theories behind writing centers parallel how writers work. Writers know that writing is a process; we also know that each of our processes is a little bit different. We find our own ways. This makes life in the classroom enormously challenging for the teachers who attempt to standardize their approach. Yes, there are the basics that we all know (e.g., prewriting and planning; drafting and discovering; revising, editing, and proofing; publishing or presenting), but in the end our jobs as teachers and editors of our students' work is to help them discover their own most effective process and to support that process with respect and care.

Later in this book I will offer a list of resources to help you and your student staff come to know more about the theory and practice involved in writing center work.

Kinds of Writing Centers

Many universities, community colleges, and a few 6th-12th grade schools offer writing centers staffed with faculty, students, and community volunteers. Turn to the Internet for virtual writing centers called OWLs (online writing labs). Though this book's focus is the student-staffed writing center, understanding the different kinds of centers will help you make an informed decision about your school's needs. In addition, we can all learn from one another. The activities and resources of community-based writing centers are models for the potential of 6th-12th grade centers; OWLs teach us about virtual feedback and using the best words to help a writer think about her work. Keep an open mind when considering the promise of various kinds of writing centers.

Faculty-Staffed Writing Centers

Some faculty-staffed writing centers have full-time specialists. Their jobs are to work in the writing center and support classroom writing across the curriculum. The Jefferson Middle School writing lab in Pennsylvania's Mt. Lebanon School District has a full-time clinician. The clinician's job is spelled out on Jefferson Middle School's website:

> What is the role of the Writing Lab Clinician? The Writing Lab Clinician is an English teacher who works full time with students and instructors in room 102. The Clinician is available to discuss problems the student is having in his or her writing and to help him or her discover solutions. The Clinician will neither write nor fix papers. The student will remain the author of his or her own document. The Clinician will, however, help the student become familiar with the writing process and strategies for revision. *Jefferson Middle School Writing Lab*

In other faculty-staffed centers, English department members serve in the writing centers. For as many periods as possible, at least one English teacher is available for conferences. On occasion, teachers from other departments volunteer for writing center duty. A teacher's writing center service usually replaces other school duties, such as study hall. Some teachers and departments simply volunteer to staff the writing center during planning periods. Just as with the student-staffed center, writing center teachers confer with students in an effort to find focus, develop ideas, revise sentences, correct technical mistakes, or put the finishing touches on a piece of writing.

The Branson School in California has a writing center that combines faculty and student feedback as well as full-class activities as revealed in the following statement from their website:

> Since feedback is an important part of the writing process, faculty members are available in the center to provide observation and coaching. Students work independently, collaboratively with other students or teachers, and collectively with their classes. Students practice and play with their writing—with their grammar, sentence structure, theses, topic sentences, spelling, revisions, diction, transitions, arguments, conclusions—before they hand in a paper. They talk; they write; they rewrite. www.branson.org/writingcenter.html

(An obvious reminder about Web addresses offered in this book: If these addresses are obsolete, use your preferred search engine to find an updated address by typing in, for example, "The Branson School Writing Center.")

Such writing centers serve students from all disciplines. One political consideration about faculty-staffed writing centers: Writing center teacher consultants will have an opportunity to enter a colleague's classroom through the student's work and accompanying conversation. This reality can be exciting for some teachers because they will have an opportunity to share the brilliance of their classrooms with colleagues. But for some teachers, having colleagues view their teaching practices through the eyes of students will be disconcerting, and they may choose not to have their students use the writing center. For a school of 1,000 students with ten to twelve English teachers, the issue surfaces of too few editors for too many students. Another reality is burdening English teachers with more reading and response to writing.

Faculty-staffed writing centers usually require students to sign up in advance. Busy, active faculty-staffed writing centers are not able to accommodate drop-in clients. Customarily, the sign-up sheets for the week are on the door of the center—students jot down their names in the time slots and, if necessary, pick up a corridor pass from their academic teacher. No matter whether the writing center is student- or faculty-staffed, most schools require a note from a student's academic teacher to leave study hall for editing help. In return, writing center faculty members may send an e-mail or note to the academic teacher about the student's visit. The note may be quite simple: "Theresa came in for a conference re: 'Understanding Wallace Stevens.'" Or, the writing center teacher may go more in depth:

> Theresa's essay on Wallace Stevens lacked a well-developed conclusion. We talked about the possibilities, and I think she has a good idea how to further develop the ending. I admired her ability to analyze Stevens's difficult poems—she must be a delight in class!

Many classroom teachers appreciate such a dialogue as it allows them to see their students, and their students' work, through the lens of another adult.

In well-wired schools, signing up may be online. A virtual calendar allows students, teachers, and administrators to view who is using the writing center and when. Such a calendar makes data collection easier and also helps with greater school-wide accountability. Administrators appreciate this immensely.

A positive dimension of the faculty-staffed writing center is that teachers outside the English department may use the services more readily. These teachers feel more comfortable with trained professionals helping their students. Furthermore, teachers from other disciplines may request a writing center teacher to visit their classes for presentations on particular kinds of writing. For instance, a science teacher may ask for assistance on correct citations for research papers, or a social studies teacher may want her students to write poems about a certain time in history. Writing center English teachers are also invited into colleagues' classrooms to confer individually with students about writing projects. In essence, the writing center faculty member partners up with the regular classroom teacher. This collaboration serves as a model for students, allows for professional conversations among faculty members, and emphasizes writing across the curriculum. For students, such team teaching adds one more adult to the classroom to help out.

OWLs: Online Writing Labs

In searching for virtual writing centers, you will see the term "OWL." Many of these sites include online dictionaries, reference materials, instructional handouts, Web design resources, and links to the homepages of other writing centers around the nation. The International Writing Centers Association (IWCA) has an online database of writing centers across the nation. Many of these sites have OWLs. Checkout the IWCA "Links to Writing Centers Online" website (http://writingcenters.org/owcdb).

E-handouts from OWLs run the gamut. For those writers who want to refresh their technical writing minds or seek out assistance, these pages stimulate thinking and serve as tutorials. Since OWLs usually are part of a college site, some of the handouts (e.g., writing a master's thesis) focus solely on a college student's needs. The following is a sampling of e-handouts found on the University of North Carolina's site that are available to writers on most OWL sites:

Writing the Paper	Statistics
Argument in Academic Writing	Transitions
Introductions & Conclusions	Writing Groups
Constructing Thesis Statements	
Getting Feedback on Writing	Grammar & Mechanics
	Articles
Logical Fallacies	MLA Citations
Organization	APA Citations
Paragraph Development	CBE Citations
Plagiarism	Commas
Reading Toward Writing	Evaluating Evidence
Tips on Assignments	Fragments & Run-ons

How to Quote

Active & Passive Voice

Battling Procrastination

Effective Proofreading

Revising Your Paper

Should I Use 'I'?

Style

Gender-Sensitive Language

Word Choice

Writing Assignments:

Application Essays

Comparison and Contrast Essays

Dissertations

Essay Exams

Literature Reviews

Poetry Explications

Writing an Honors Thesis

Writing a Review

Writing Speeches

© 2005, UNC-CH Writing Center, University of North Carolina at Chapel Hill
(www.unc.edu/depts/wcweb/handouts)

OWL sites prove to be useful resources for any writer. When a student is working on a weekend or late at night and needs assistance with any number of writing issues, an OWL can provide helpful information. Moreover, such sites can be incredibly useful for 6th-12th grade writing center staff as a ready resource and part of their training.

My friend Carol Ellis directed The Writing Center at Claremont Graduate University in California. Their website is rich and complete with many helpful connections and resources (www.cgu.edu/pages/726.asp). In addition, their staff accepts online e-mail submissions of up to fifty pages! Online tutorial response remains a topic of much discussion among writing center personnel at the post-secondary level as witnessed by the extensive dialogues within the various Discussion Forums of the International Writing Centers Association (IWCA) (www.writingcenters.org/board/index.php). The consensus seems to be that online responses don't match the quality of face-to-face tutorials.

With my editor, Anne, face-to-face is inordinately helpful and fun; truth be known, however, we do virtually all of our manuscript discussions online. At first, e-mailed conversations left me feeling a bit empty—probably because I enjoyed the personal time with Anne and my questions were answered as they surfaced. However, over time, we have become good at e-communicating. Why? Two reasons: We're professionals and we have a twenty-five-year relationship as editor-writer and friends. In Anne's editorial practice, ninety-nine percent of her work with authors is via e-mail and/or phone calls.

Some of the writing center staff members who wrote in to the WCENTER Digest (02.26.05) said that they encouraged students to e-mail their papers and then call on the phone to discuss the work. For some nontraditional students who can't easily make it to campus, this kind of service is phenomenal. It makes sense to me that some small amount of editorial work in a 6th-12th grade writing center takes place online. Yes, such discussions will challenge both writer and student-editor, but I do believe such a stretch can be meaningful.

Among the many OWL sites, the Purdue University OWL "Family of Sites" is considered a model. Check out their site by going to their webpage (http://owl.english.purdue.edu/writinglab), or using your favorite search engine, type in "The Writing Lab at Purdue." Other popular links include The Writing Center at University of Notre Dame and Salt Lake Community College Student Writing Center.

University-Affiliated Writing Centers

Connecting a 6th-12th grade writing center to a university makes good sense on many levels. Such a collaboration can prove beneficial to both writing centers. One mutual benefit is having university consultants train secondary school students. When the local university writing center personnel trained our high school editors, the university director spoke and then a number of his writing center consultants worked with our students one on one. My students left this one-day workshop with new knowledge and a greater understanding of, and appreciation for, their role in the writing center. As for the university staff, teaching the high school students helped, too. As one of the university students said, "Explaining my job and talking about the process I use was challenging. Jamie asked great questions—she kept making me think about what I was doing. I probably learned more than she did!"

A daily or weekly connection may be possible for 6th-12th grade schools in close proximity to a university writing center. One such connection could be having university tutors serve as assistant directors of a school's writing center—some college students will need practicum experiences as part of their work toward becoming certified as teachers. Others will simply want to volunteer. For university students, this experience enhances their resume and helps in their job searches. Some university students are paid through work-study for their work at school writing centers. Others, usually graduate students, do their university research at school sites.

The Philadelphia Writing Centers Project (PWCP), a site of the National Writing Project (NWP), partnered area high schools with local universities. The PWCP grant funded school-based academic writing centers and ongoing professional development opportunities for school staff while assisting in the maintenance of a writing center. You might check with your local National Writing Project site (www.writingproject.org/) to see what might be possible.

Columbia University's Teachers College offers after-school writing center programs in New York City. Columbia's fee-based program offers one-on-one tutoring opportunities as well as three-to-four-hour workshops for small groups of six to eight. Our student-staffed writing center offered a number of after-school programs. (More on these programs later in the book.)

For the 6th-12th grade writing center, an affiliation with a college or university can bring a level of prestige and legitimacy to the operation. I believe that more secondary school teachers encourage students to use the writing center if the university has a hand in it. Such a school-university partnership also attracts promising editors from the high school population.

Community-Based Writing Centers

San Francisco's "826 Valencia" could be called the ultimate in community writing centers. Recognized in 2003 by the National Council of Teachers of English, 826 Valencia serves school children throughout the city, as they explain on their website (www.826valencia.org):

> Simply put, 826 Valencia helps students, ages 8–18, to develop their writing skills. Whether the students are working in the realm of fiction, nonfiction, or English as a second language, we are here to help them explore their love of writing. We offer free drop-in tutoring, workshops, and storytelling. We also help students create their own story collections, zines, and other publications.

826 Valencia also hosts seminars for aspiring or developing writers in the Bay Area. These monthly three-hour workshops serve as a fundraiser for 826 Valencia and are put on *pro bono* by a panel of Bay Area writers, editors, and agents. The website's promotional material cites that the "emphasis will be on the practicalities of getting one's work published, finding agents, developing and sticking with good work habits, getting valuable feedback—generally, all the strategies important to a writer's life."

826 Valencia also hosts school field trips, loans its tutors to classrooms, and works with students on creative writing, journalism, film, design, photo manipulation, comics, and publishing on the Web. To check out the events calendar, go to their main website and click on to "Upcoming Events."

Do Not Feel Limited

Looking at the variety of writing centers should encourage you to develop the kind of writing center that fits best for your school, district, and community. Do not feel limited. No matter the kind of writing center you may end up with, I am convinced just having a space devoted to writing will raise awareness and conversation, and thereby improve writing at your school.

CHAPTER TWO

Planning and Organizing

One of the first steps in developing a 6th-12th grade writing center will be holding discussions with your English/language arts colleagues about the concept. Your colleagues' support is vital. If some of these teachers are recent graduates, they may be familiar with university writing centers. Perhaps they were writing center staff or had friends who were. Or, perhaps as part of their English studies, they were required to use their university's writing center. Since university writing centers are often housed in English departments, it's not unusual for English education majors to be acquainted with them in one way or another. Your new colleagues may be important resources and advocates as you begin your work to establish a writing center at your school.

I spent a year researching, planning, and sharing the writing center idea. Half way through the year I composed "A Prospectus: The Mountain Valley High School Writing Center" (see Figure 2-1) and shared it with my English colleagues and the high school administration. I thought I had done a good job keeping my English colleagues informed, but when the final proposal was approved in June by the principal, the superintendent, and the school board, a couple of my colleagues were unhappy. I spoke about the writing center at every monthly department meeting during the yearlong planning phase. I passed out literature and flyers from the nearby university writing center. In hindsight, though, I now realize I should have invited the university writing center director to a department meeting, at least in part, to take the focus off me.

During the planning phase I was careful not to assume that I would automatically be selected as the writing center director—though I am sure that people figured I would apply. In retrospect, my speaking in department meetings about "whoever would be the writing center director" probably came across as artificial or disingenuous. It sure sounds it when I write the words now.

In the end I know what bothered my unhappy colleagues the most: The new writing center director would be released from teaching two courses.

A Prospectus:
The Mountain Valley High School Writing Center

The Concept:
A Writing Center is a place where students and staff go to obtain assistance with their writing or to work on a writing project. Trained Writing Center staff members aid clients in all phases of the writing process, including prewriting, drafting, revising, editing, and publishing. A Writing Center has a number of computers available. The main objective of a Writing Center is to help writers become more effective writers.

Staff:
A member of the English Department will serve as the director of The Writing Center, and we propose a two-course release. The director will be assisted by another member of the faculty, with a one-course release, and by selected students who have demonstrated a solid understanding of the writing process and who are good communicators. These student-editors, or tutors, will receive extensive and ongoing training in the teaching of writing. Student-editors will take their English class from The Writing Center director in a specially designed class. Volunteer staff members will be solicited from the high school staff and from the greater community.

Hours of Operation:
The Writing Center will be open every school morning at 7:15 a.m. During the course of the regular school day, The Writing Center will be open each academic period and lunchtime, but not during Advisory Time. Depending on need and staffing, The Writing Center will remain open after school. Ideally, The Writing Center will be open two evenings a week (Tuesdays and Thursdays) and, again, according to need and staffing, Sunday evenings from 6 p.m. to 7:30 p.m. Our hope is to have the MVHS Library open during the evening hours as well.

Client Usage:
Clients may drop in to The Writing Center and be referred by a teacher or parent/caregiver. Like the MVHS Library, The Writing Center will have to restrict the number of student and staff clients at any one time based on space, staff presence, and computer availability.

Special Offerings:
The Writing Center will offer special courses in writing such as How to Write a Letter of Inquiry for a Summer Job, Fiction Writing, Vocabulary Enhancement, and Writing a College Application Essay. The Writing Center will also offer an ongoing SAT Seminar and an evening of readings by professional writers. Another exciting idea is to run a symposium on writing for the faculty and staff. For example, The Writing Center might invite a member of the math department of The University of Maine at Farmington to discuss his or her use of writing in the classroom. The Writing Center might be open on a weeknight to the general community to assist in certain writing projects (e.g., resumes, letters of inquiry); this type of outreach program would be valuable to the school and to the community.

Figure 2–1, Writing Center Prospectus (front page)

National Council of Teachers of English Position Statement

On Writing Centers
1987
NCTE Annual Business Meeting in Los Angeles, California

Background
In this resolution, NCTE members recognized the important contribution writing centers have made to the success of many students at all levels of education. Be it therefore

Resolution
Resolved, that the National Council of Teachers of English endorse the principle that the establishment of a writing center should be a long-term commitment on the part of an institution, including stable budgeting and full academic status; and that NCTE widely publish this resolution to its affiliates and other professional organizations and refer institutions to the full text of the "Position Statement on Professional Concerns of Writing Center Directors" published in *The Writing Center Journal* 6 (1985).

Figure 2-1, Writing Center Prospectus (back page)

From the very beginning, the course release information was a part of the writing center proposal passed out to department members, but the reality never hit home until the final go-ahead came through. Looking back, perhaps I should have kept teaching the two courses and directed the writing center in lieu of more traditional teacher duties (e.g., cafeteria duty or study hall). I'm not sure if I could have been effective teaching a full load and directing the new center as a second-year English teacher, but I know that there was bitterness because of my schedule. As a result of those feelings, I went back to teaching five courses plus a duty (a study hall) the following year, and then a year later I took on a sixth course along with my writing center duties. I don't recommend this schedule, especially in the initial year of operation.

This is all to say that you can plan and communicate, hand out flyers and seek input until the proverbial cows come home, but you're never certain of your colleagues' ultimate response or what might trigger that response. Of course, you're the best judge of your own department, but I think you must keep uppermost in your mind that the writing center concept at the secondary level is a radical change on many fronts—this change can cause challenges.

Fortify Your Background in Writing Instruction

Writing center pedagogy connects with theories of writing instruction. For some new writing center directors, it may be helpful to think about and study writing instruction in the context of the classroom, the school, and the district. Two sources really help bring writing instruction into focus for me. First, *Because Writing Matters: Improving Student Writing in Our Schools* (2003) by the National Writing Project and Carl Nagin is a smart book that does a solid job of putting writing in context. This book offers a global picture of the teaching of writing in our schools. The book also includes sources and research about how students learn to write, what schools and school districts must do to help support effective writing instruction, and step-by-step recommendations for developing effective K-12 writing programs. The following outlines the key points of *Because Writing Matters*:

- Improving writing is crucial to learning in all subject areas, not just English.
- Writing instruction should begin in the earliest grades.
- Reading and writing are reinforcing literacy skills and need to be taught together.
- Learning to write requires frequent, supportive practice.
- Students have diverse abilities and instructional needs, and so teachers must use multiple strategies to improve students' writing.
- Effective writing instruction pays attention to both the product and processes of writing.
- Writing should be taught in school much as it is practiced by professional writers: that is, students should write for authentic purposes to real audiences.
- Students face ongoing challenges in their writing development and need practice with diverse writing tasks to improve.
- Simply assigning more writing is not enough. Teachers must teach students such skills as how to organize thoughts, develop ideas, and revise for clarity.
- An effective writing assignment does more than ask students to report what they have read or experienced. It engages students in such processes as problem solving, reflecting, analyzing, and imagining so that they can think critically about what they have read or experienced.
- Schools cannot improve writing without teachers and administrators who value, understand, and practice writing themselves.

- Teachers and schools need to develop common expectations for good writing across grade levels and subject areas.
- Schools and districts need to develop fair and authentic writing assessments that are aligned with high standards and reflect student progress beyond single-test evaluations.
- Effective school-wide writing programs involve the entire faculty and are developed across the curriculum.
- Schools and districts need to offer professional development opportunities in teaching writing to all faculty.

Reprinted with permission from the National Writing Project. "Key Points" from *Because Writing Matters*, NWP Press Room at www.writingproject.org.

Second, NCTE *Beliefs about the Teaching of Writing* by the Writing Study Group of the NCTE Executive Committee (November 2004) has spot-on statements about writing and our classrooms. The following eleven points highlight the overarching beliefs—an eighteen-page statement may be found on the NCTE website (www.ncte.org):

1. Everyone has the capacity to write, writing can be taught, and teachers can help students become better writers.
2. People learn to write by writing.
3. Writing is a process.
4. Writing is a tool for thinking.
5. Writing grows out of many different purposes.
6. Conventions of finished and edited texts are important to readers and therefore to writers.
7. Writing and reading are related.
8. Writing has a complex relationship to talk.
9. Literate practices are embedded in complicated social relationships.
10. Composing occurs in different modalities and technologies.
11. Assessment of writing involves complex, informed, human judgment.

Having this language will help build your reputation as an emerging authority on writing within your school.

Introducing the Writing Center Concept
to your Department Colleagues

The following suggestions may help you introduce the writing center concept
to your English/language arts colleagues at a department meeting:

1. Discuss college/university writing centers.

You may wish to have data available on the number of students from your
school who move on to post-secondary education. In virtually every case,
these students will have an opportunity to utilize a writing center or a
learning center at the next level of school. According to the Council for
Higher Education Accreditation Fact Sheet #1 for 2003, there were 6,421
accredited post-secondary institutions. In an e-mail discussion with the co-
editor of *The Writing Center Journal*, MIT's Neal Lerner speculates "[t]hat
every one of those institutions has some form of writing support/writing
tutoring, more likely in a learning center than in a writing center" adding
that "Student Support Services is a required component for accreditation." The East Central Writing Centers Association alone reports its
membership to be 546 post-secondary writing centers in their region (IL,
IN, KY, OH, PA, and WV). In fact, ECWCA has a full directory of their
members on their website at the following Internet address:
www.marietta.edu/%7Emcwrite/eastcentraldirectory.htm

2. Tour a model OWL using a digital projector.

These websites are impressive. Many of your colleagues will be amazed and
will appreciate the information as a resource with their own students.
Many of us struggle to bring technology into the classroom; using an
OWL is one small way that can have big benefits, not the least of which is
an emphasis on writing. As mentioned, the Writing Lab at Purdue University is a model. Also, check out your nearby colleges and universities to
see if their writing centers have OWLs.

3. Share the following article:

"The High School Writing Lab/Center: A Dialogue" by Speiser and Farrell in *The High School Writing Center: Establishing and Maintaining One* (Farrell, 1989, pp. 9–22). This conversation examines the ins and outs of
writing centers at the high school level. It provides a historical context and

reveals the political issues surrounding writing centers. Even though the book was published in 1989, the realities of writing centers are well depicted in this chapter. The conversation between Speiser and Farrell raises important points and will most likely provide the genesis of some of your department's dialogues. Using this article gives teachers the kind of background knowledge they'll appreciate—they will certainly feel more a part of the process of creating a writing center by reading this piece.

4. Invite a university or 6th-12th grade writing center director to talk.

This kind of first-hand information is invaluable for your colleagues. Putting a face beyond your own to the writing center idea is helpful. For my students, having college writing center staff talk to them about tutoring was important on many levels. Perhaps your guest could bring along one or two students. It may be helpful if you could find a former student from your school who now works in a college writing center. This input personalizes and connects.

5. Gather a list of issues with your colleagues surrounding the development of a writing center and discuss that list thoroughly.

Professionals appreciate hearing all sides of issues—with writing centers there are the positives and the challenges. Be up front and talk them through thoroughly.

6. Share the following article:

"The Concept of a Writing Center" by Muriel Harris, a SLATE (Support for the Learning and Teaching of English) statement from NCTE (see Appendix A, page 151).

7. Distribute the 1987 National Council of Teachers of English Position Statement on Writing Centers (see Figure 2-1, page 19).

Again, working with your English/language arts colleagues is critical. If the majority of your colleagues support the writing center idea, or at the very least won't create roadblocks, your work will be easier. The keys to success include keeping everyone informed and including everyone in the conversations. Soliciting input from critics will be vital. Knowing their arguments will help you frame responses.

The conversations that emerge from these first steps of creating a writing center will be brilliant, inasmuch as writing will be discussed in ways you may never have thought possible. When working with your English/ language arts colleagues, try to keep your emotions out of the equation. Try to listen with detachment and accept that some teachers' objections to the development of a writing center have to do with the fear of the unknown, a lack of confidence about a teacher's own classroom writing practices, or the simple fact that a teacher feels excluded from the process. Remember: You can have as many assistant or associate writing center directors as there are English teachers in your school! Also recognize that the institution of school and its players—parents/caregivers, teachers, principals, and even students—struggle with change.

Working with Your Principal

By necessity, administrators have a global view of school. They will want to know how writing centers promote writing across the curriculum, whether the presence of a writing center improves test scores, what the research is on peer tutoring, whether a writing center will fit into the day-to-day of the school's operation, and of course, the bottom line: How much will it cost and where will it be housed?

I'd suggest arranging a fifteen-minute meeting to introduce the idea. Showcase representative writing center books, articles, facts, and figures; much of this material you can collect from a local university writing center director or from the International Writing Centers Association webpage cited earlier. You might place selections of this material in a one-inch, three-ring binder with a concise (one-paragraph) opening statement. This professional presentation piece—like a view book or a marketing proposal—will do much to attract your busy principal. If at this point you have the support of your department, it might be a good idea to have a group statement, signed by all and at the front of the document, agreeing to explore the possibilities of a writing center.

The following represent suggestions for organizing information for your building principal—be careful not to inundate her with lots of reading material. One idea: Include interested department colleagues in the development of this packet—make them a part of the founding efforts of the writing center. Divide up the responsibilities into small assignments and ask your teaching friends if they would like to be involved. Again, some of the information can be gathered in a very few minutes from the Internet.

Principal's Packet

Introduction: Include an introductory statement about writing centers and explain the various kinds and their influence at the university level. Include the 1987 National Council of Teachers of English Position Statement on Writing Centers and recommendations from "The Neglected 'R': The Need for a Writing Revolution" of The National Commission on Writing in America's Schools and Colleges (April 2003). Two of the Commission's recommendations state the following:

- The amount of time and resources devoted to student writing should be at least doubled.
- Writing should be taught in all subjects and at all grade levels.

Explain, too, that the Commission recognizes the challenges facing K-12 teachers. "Elementary school teachers typically face a single class of twenty-five to thirty-five students.... Many upper-level teachers, on the other hand, face between 120 to 200 students, weekly if not daily. Teachers of English (or history or biology) who ask simply for a weekly one-page paper are immediately overwhelmed with the challenge of reading, responding to, and evaluating what their request produces" (p. 20).

The Commission's second report, "Writing: A Ticket to Work...Or a Ticket Out, A Survey of Business Leaders" (September 2004) includes critical information for principals whose students head off to post-secondary schools or enter the job market. Citing the major findings would give authority to your work. Those findings include the following:

- People who cannot write and communicate clearly will not be hired and are unlikely to last long enough to be considered for promotion. Half of responding companies reported that they take writing into consideration when hiring professional employees and when making promotion decisions. "In most cases, writing ability could be your ticket in...or it could be your ticket out," said one respondent. Commented another, "You can't move up without writing skills."
- Two-thirds of salaried employees in large American companies have some writing responsibility. "All employees must have writing ability.... Manufacturing documentation, operating procedures, reporting problems, lab safety, waste-disposal operations—all have to be crystal clear," said one human resource director.
- Eighty percent or more of the companies in the services and the finance, insurance, and real estate (FIRE) sectors—the corporations with

greatest employment growth potential—assess writing during hiring. "Applicants who provide poorly written letters wouldn't likely get an interview," commented one insurance executive.

- More than forty percent of responding firms offer or require training for salaried employees with writing deficiencies. "We're likely to send out 200–300 people annually for skills upgrade courses like 'business writing' or 'technical writing,'" said one respondent.

A third report, "Writing: A Powerful Message from State Government," appeared on July 5, 2005. All three reports are available through the website of The National Commission on Writing in America's Schools and Colleges (www.writingcommission.org).

You may end this section to your administrator with a statement similar to the following: "Clearly, teachers need more assistance in reading and responding to student writing. We believe a writing center can help."

Rationale for a Writing Center: In this section of the Principal's Packet, include statistics on your school's writing achievements and scores. Comment on the English teachers' class loads, if that's an issue (remembering that NCTE suggests teachers at high school have a load of 80:1), and how this inhibits the kind of genuine writing instruction necessary. Again, refer to the "The Neglected 'R'" and its statement that "[t]eachers of English (or history or biology) who ask simply for a weekly one-page paper are immediately overwhelmed with the challenge of reading, responding to, and evaluating what their request produces" (p. 20).

Statements of Support: Including letters of support assures your principal that you've done your homework.

English/language arts colleagues: A short paragraph signed by your colleagues stating that they agree to investigate the possibility of a writing center.

Key personnel in your school: Have discussions with key school personnel in school about writing centers and ask if they would allow you to investigate the possibility of a writing center. Include a note from them.

Local university writing center directors: Principals want the best for their students. Knowing that such a thing as a writing center exists at the next level will connect with them in a meaningful way. Most university or college writing center directors will be thrilled to hear about your adventure and will send along a letter or an e-mail of support in an instant.

Principals whose schools have writing centers: With a bit of research, you'll be able to find out which schools in your state or region have writing centers. Contact the writing center directors, explain what you're up to, and ask if they could supply quotations from their principal and themselves. It may be helpful to use schools more like your own.

Former students: No doubt, some of your students have gone on to college and utilized and/or worked in a writing center. Including their stories would be an important addition to this document. Tracking these students down could be a matter of identifying those students who went off to college as English or education majors. Your English or guidance department colleagues may know the names of such students.

Other materials for the Principal's Packet: Include information pieces from the International Writing Center Association. Include IWCA items such as *The Writing Center Journal*, the *Writing Lab Newsletter*, and "Guide to Writing Center Publications" (Kearcher and Patchan, 2003), from the association's home page. Including a printout of the home page itself makes sense, too. (http://writingcenters.org/index.php)

Include three printed home pages from university OWLs. It might be a good idea to include the home page from a highly valued college or university near your school or in your state.

Finally, you may wish to include all three reports from The National Commission on Writing in America's Schools and Colleges. Once again, copies of the reports may be downloaded at www.writingcommission.org.

Spreading the Word

Once you've enticed your principal, make a list of other critical constituents. Outline a plan of approach while realizing that much of what you have gathered for your principal and English/language arts colleagues will be useful with these groups. You won't need to address all of these groups in the planning stages. Depending on your school and school system, critical players in the initial stages may include the curriculum coordinator, the superintendent, potential university affiliations, potential business partners, and your school staff.

Entire school staff: Include everyone: custodians, guidance counselors, athletic coaches, other faculty, lunch room personnel, school resource officer, social workers, school nurse...

Students: If your school is wired and you have access to sites for posting school-wide messages, you may wish to post several OWL sites as an introduction to writing centers. Mention that you'll be seeking writing center personnel in the not-too distant future. You and/or students who have shown an interest in the writing center may wish to put up posters. You'll want to share information about the various services that will be available (e.g., SAT seminars).

Parents/caregivers, PTA, PTO, or the parent advisory council: Many involved parents/caregivers hope their child(ren) will head off to post-secondary school. Knowing that most colleges and universities have writing centers and that their child should know how to use one may be enough to capture their support.

Potential business partnerships: Don't sell this constituency short. Large and small businesses may like the idea of collaborating in the writing center adventure. Perhaps one would sponsor the writing center brochure or provide money for writing center resource books or a guest writers' series.

Potential university affiliations: University writing centers will champion your cause. Include them!

Superintendent of schools: Your principal may be the right person to introduce the writing center concept to his or her supervisor, the superintendent. You may offer to supply a second informational portfolio such as the one you provided the principal.

Curriculum coordinator: Many districts have curriculum coordinators. You will want to include this person as soon as you have the nod from your language arts colleagues and the principal.

School board: You may have to present to the school board, but you'll want to wait until you get the OK from your superintendent and principal. As you know, the hierarchy in schools is alive and well.

K-6 school staff: K-6 staff regularly have their students work in groups, from literature circles to writers' workshops. Creating a student-staffed writing center at the high school will be seen as a popular decision among these kid-centered professionals.

The media: Newspaper reporters are always looking for stories. Some newspaper writers with English degrees may have been a part of writing centers, and they may wish to add their expertise! We had one article per year in the local newspapers about the writing center. In addition, your district and school may have newsletters in which you could place photographs and articles.

The general public: Once the center is up and running, and you have had an article in the local newspaper, you may wish to have an evening affair for the public with an author talk, resume building, or computer training.

The Politics of Writing Centers

It is a fundamental truth that creating and maintaining a writing center in a school is a political act. The presence of a writing center changes the landscape of a school and creates a paradigm shift (see Figure 2–2). There's even an award-winning book titled *The Politics of Writing Centers* (2001) edited by Jane Nelson, University of Wyoming and Kathy Evertz, University of Wyoming. Though this book focuses on the college writing center, you'll hear truths that cross over to 6th-12th grade centers.

Depending on your writing center's philosophy of staffing, you may have "weaker" writers acting as student-editors for "stronger" writers. This happened in our center and the results created rich conversations in my

The Paradigm Shift

Without a Writing Center:	*With a Writing Center:*
Teachers teach students in their classrooms	Students leave their classrooms to confer with tutors in the writing center
Teachers edit student papers	Teachers, students, and others confer with students about their papers
One or two revisions of a paper	Multiple revisions of a paper
Teacher as expert	Students and teachers as experts
Homogenous grouping	Heterogeneous grouping

Figure 2–2, The Paradigm Shift

classroom and among my colleagues. To some of my colleagues, the notion of less capable student writers assisting more capable student writers didn't seem feasible. During these discussions I used the following examples from my own experience.

I've written four young adult novels—two have been published. One part of my writing process is to ask a few teenagers to read a complete draft and offer feedback. Their words help me authenticate my story and stay true to my young adult audience. True, sometimes the teenagers' comments are confounding, but all-in-all I learn a lot by listening and sorting through the comments. My colleagues then counter: "You're a professional writer with the ability to negotiate the variety of comments about your writing. But many student writers won't have the savvy and experience to take what they can from a classmate who may offer poor suggestions."

My answer is in this story. Joshua spent his 9th through 12th grade years in my high school English classroom. His best friend for two of those years was Anthony, an eclectic young man with an impressive academic record. Joshua and Anthony shared their stories and poems with one another—they collaborated on a book project together regarding my young adult novel, *The Mosquito Test* (1994). Joshua worked with other students, too. He served as a cast member in classroom plays, an editor to their work, and joined into discussions about our classroom themes.

Joshua lives with Down's syndrome—he is a most original and uninhibited improvisational actor. And funny? He could crack up a classroom with a simple tilt of the head, or quiet us with a sensitive rendition of Elvis's "Love Me Tender." Joshua also possessed an attribute as an editor that, well, perhaps only he could get away with: He told the dead-honest truth about a student writer's work. When a classmate read Joshua a short story or poem that didn't keep his interest, he'd simply say, "This is boring." When a classmate's writing confused Joshua, he'd say, "I don't get it." Yes, at first the writer would chuckle and kid with Joshua, but then, always, there was the wondering.

You see, Joshua loved good stories and we all knew this. He was a huge fan of *The Lord of the Rings* series and presented book talks on a wide range of other books that he had enjoyed. True, Joshua was not a sophisticated writer, but he knew good stories. In the end, Joshua's words made these young writers think. Indeed, he did what effective editors do: He helped writers think about and reconsider their writing in the midst of their revising.

No matter how you staff your writing center, those of us who confer with writers—those of us who serve as editors, consultants, or tutors—understand the subtlety and mystery of the craft. Donald M. Murray (2004) calls this subtlety the mysterious "black box" of writing. In addition, you may be an effective writer, yet struggle as an editor. The political aspect of writing centers has a positive side, but it won't always feel that way. The wide variety of conversations focused on the philosophies or pedagogy of writing, teaching, or learning will raise critical questions and help people learn. Don't be put off by this aspect of developing your center.

On Being a Volunteer Faculty-Director

On average as a volunteer director, I spent about one hundred and fifty hours a year on writing center work. Honestly, this estimate is a wild guess. Some of that time came from corresponding with future editors in the summertime. Some was spent in developing brochures, training editors, keeping and publishing statistics, editing pieces of work, chatting with visitors interested in secondary writing centers, and fielding questions and complaints from colleagues, students, and administrators. That's right, even though I volunteered, as the writing center director I still took the flak. I used that feedback, and a lot of it was valid criticism, to improve our writing center. As director you can't take things personally. That's not always easy if you're volunteering, but in the end you'll see that the effort is worth the occasional heartache.

How are Writing Center Directors Selected? Faculty-directors in 6th-12th grades usually select themselves. They are motivated people who understand the power, potential, and promise of writing center work. These folks have an understanding of the need for writing centers in their school and they welcome student-to-student, writer-to-writer discussions. At this point in time, directing a 6th-12th grade writing center is a calling. Student-staffed writing centers may benefit from having faculty co-directors and multiple assistant directors from across the curriculum. School-wide support of the writing center concept can develop through involvement.

CHAPTER THREE

Staffing and Training

Maybe in a perfect world, all writers would have their own ready auditor—a teacher, a classmate, a roommate, an editor—who would not only listen but draw them out, ask them questions they would not think to ask themselves. A writing center is an institutional response to this need.

—Stephen North, "The Idea of a Writing Center" (1984)

By year three, after our writing center was fully established, any student could select the English course, "The Writing Center," and work as a student-editor. This course counted as a regular English credit and fit into the typical sequence of English courses. Eventually, this heterogeneous, cross-aged collection of kids occupied three of my six classes. At the writing center's peak, about sixty student-editors from my classes worked in The Writing Center. A few students in my other traditional English classes volunteered in the center for extra credit. Other English teachers' students volunteered for credit, too. At this point we had more than enough student-editors to staff every period of every day, including before and after school.

Over the years, I recruited former writing center students. I found it especially important to find highly organized students to serve as directors of our center. Usually, seniors were student-directors and then we'd have a couple of assistant directors from the junior class. This arrangement helped with The Writing Center continuity and, to be honest, lightened my load as faculty-director. The more effective the student-directors, the more fun I could have with other English class or Writing Center projects.

When a colleague or another student would recommend a potential staff member, I'd send a letter to the student's home to introduce the concept (see Figure 3-1). I sent a letter for a couple of reasons. First, with the wonder of e-mail, kids rarely receive personal letters at home anymore and this letter was one way to show the importance of the request. Second, sometimes asking kids face to face in school is an exercise in quick, incomplete conversations. With a letter, students could think about the opportunity and then find a time to come talk with me.

Dear Kelly,

Several people, both student and faculty colleagues, have recommended you to me. I am always searching for students who would enjoy working as student-editors in The Writing Center. I'm wondering whether this would be of interest to you.

Briefly, editors work as volunteers in The Writing Center or in my room (109) during study halls. These folks meet with fellow writers—students, faculty and staff, and community members—to offer assistance during all phases of the composing process. Some editors offer theme "ideas"; others work on the overall format of the piece; still others look closely at paragraph and sentence development. Frequently, in the final phase of composing, The Writing Center student-editors are used for grammatical/technical edits.

One thing. Editors are not expected to be "super human" or perfect. Each student does the best she or he can. One thing we don't do is write the paper (story, poem, or essay) for the student. We also don't take the blame if students don't get the grade they believe they deserve. All final decisions about a paper are the writer's. Period.

What's the pay off, you ask? Good question. First, the experience. The more you edit fellow writers' work, the better writer you become. That's pretty obvious, I'm sure. Writing is a powerful way to learn. Second, you get paid $25,000 a year. Yes, Kelly, I'm joking.

Third, your name is listed in one of my sophomore classes. So, if you edit for The Writing Center and keep a log of those edits, you receive extra credit (1-4 points on your quarter grade depending on the amount of editing) toward your English grade. Also, we ask that editors read and write during the summer; this beefs up your portfolio for first quarter. See the enclosed letters that I have already sent to next year's editors for further information.

And finally, virtually every college and university in the United States has a writing center or a learning center that staffs student-editors. For a number of my former student colleagues who worked in the MVHS center, this experience has gotten them a job! But more, college admissions people are impressed with the fact that a student volunteered to work with other students in such a learning situation. The Writing Center is a unique idea for the high school level.

So, did I sell it? If you have questions, talk with folks like Lincoln M., Sydney R., Mike A., Donna I., or others who have volunteered in past years.

Feel free to call or write me if you have any questions. Thank you for considering this position. I hope you're having a restful summer filled with barbecue pig-outs, beach frolics, Coos Canyon escapes, OOB rendezvous, and a bit of reading and writing!

Warmly, your soon-to-be loving English teacher,
Rich Kent

Figure 3-1, Writing Center Staff Recruitment Letter

If your school is typical, and by that I mean heavily tracked with honors, college-bound, noncollege-bound, AP, and so forth, you will probably want to begin the center with a cadre of competent student-editors. By competent I suppose I mean good students who write well—and as I mentioned previously, these kids should be likeable and welcoming.

Teaching the Writing Center Staff

In the most productive author-editor relationship, the editor, like a good dance partner who neither leads nor follows but anticipates and trusts, can help the writer find her way back into the work, can cajole another revision, contemplate the deeper themes, or supply the seamless transition, the telling detail.

—Paula Gillespie & Neal Lerner, 2000, p. 6

Teaching writing center personnel to conduct effective discussions with writers is a process that parallels teaching young writers to write. There are, however, a number of books on the market specifically to help students become more effective editors, consultants, or tutors. I'll include a list at the end of this chapter.

If you develop an English class, or an elective class, specifically for writing center students, you will have ample opportunity to work with your students. As I mentioned in the first chapter, the account of my experience with such classes may be found in my books *Room 109: The Promise of a Portfolio Classroom* (1997) and *Beyond Room 109: Developing Independent Study Projects* (2000). If you do not offer a course, you may wish to host a workshop just before school begins, scatter sessions throughout the summer, or delay the opening of the center and have workshops during the first few week of the school year. Do whatever seems to work for your students and you.

If possible, have a meeting prior to the end of school (see Figure 3-2, Memo to Student-Editors). Your staff information forms could help you determine when training would work best for your student-editors (see Figure 3-3). Because we had a class for writing center student-editors (and because I took courses and worked during my summers), I didn't have summer sessions for student-editors. However, I did stay in touch with my future students.

Summer Work for Writing Center Students

Each summer I wrote and mailed eight newsy letters to my future writing center students (see Figure 3-4). It was the same letter to each student. Their assignment was to write back (see Figure 3-5). I would always answer one of their letters with a personal post card. Letter writing helped me come to know my students as writers and helped them come to know me as a teacher and writer. I did ask for letters, not e-mail, because letter writing is more formal and, generally speaking, helps students settle into a more thoughtful mode. In addition, some student-editors chose to write short stories, essays, or poems; some kept journals. Any summer writing or reading counted toward class credit during the coming school year.

The Writing Center @ Mountain Valley High School

TO: Writing Center Students
FR: Rich Kent, The Writing Center
RE: Organization Meeting, Period 6
DT: 7 June 1990

Here is a list of items that we will need to discuss during our upcoming 6th period meeting. Please take time to peruse them.

- *Your responsibilities as a member of The Writing Center Staff*: It's important for you to know that you are not Superwoman or Superman when it comes to your work in the writing center.
- *Word processing*: You need to know how to compose on a word processor.
- *Summer reading*: "We read to learn how to write and write to learn how to read"—I'll have a large selection of summer books available at our meeting.
- *Summer writing*: One of the ways to keep up with your writing is through letters; I'd like eight.
- *Our seminar*: We need to figure out what period we will have our seminar next year.
- *Pre-school workshop*: Let's try to meet for a few hours just before school begins to do some planning.
- *Study Hall*: Please bring your next year's class schedule with you.
- *England in the spring*: Once again, I'm coaching the state soccer team in England during April break. If you'd like to come along to take in the sights, speak with me.

Figure 3-2, Memo to Student-Editors

Writing Center Staff Information

Name_____ Grade _____ Homeroom_____

Home Phone_____

Address_____

Summer Phone_____

Parents/Caregivers' Names_____

Title of Writing Sample (Attach drafts, if possible)_____

Two Teacher References (one an English teacher)_____

If we were to have optional summer training sessions, what might work for you?

I'm away for the summer   _____ (X if appropriate)

_____Evenings, specifically _____

_____Days, specifically _____

Computer Abilities:

_____ *Novice*: Word process, search websites, use the basics (e.g., spell-check)

_____ *Accomplished*: insert charts in documents, make brochures, use a variety of programs

_____ *Wizard*: I can do just about anything you need, including iMovie, create Webpages

After high school I plan to...

_____

_____

(Use back if necessary)

Figure 3-3, Staff Information Form

Friday, June 18, 1993

My Dear Writing Center Student Colleagues,

It's the last day of school and the corridors are empty. Really, not much has changed. The teachers' room is overflowing with Dunkin Donuts while the grading machine in the office whizzes away averaging final assessments. A couple of students pound furiously on the computers in The Writing Center: reflecting and thinking, reflecting and thinking.

Kiesman is going bonkers because he hasn't had a class in a week; Mr. Sassi is running up and down the corridors looking for audio visual equipment; Mr. Blackman is warming up the grills for an end-of-year barbecue; Maddy is typing and laughing, typing and laughing.... It's true, not much has changed even though you are all gone.

I'm off on a tour through Canada and who knows where with my bike and truck. I'll be back around the first of July. Unfortunately, I'm unable to write each of you personal letters in response to your eight letters this summer—that would be 120 letters. I will, however, write periodic letters such as this one. Each letter will contain some rambling for you to ponder. If they don't really seem "ponderable," well, don't.... It's as simple as that. I'll do my best to write each of you a post card.

I'm including a piece by Robert Fulghum entitled "All I really need to know I learned in kindergarten." No doubt you've read this before, but you might like to take a closer look. Then again, you might not. That's okay.

Here's to you all...read a little and write a little—enjoy the change of pace.

YLET (Your Loving English Teacher),
Rich Kent

Figure 3-4, Summer Letter to The Writing Center Staff

Dear Mr. Kent,

Something happened yesterday that changed my life. It all started when I stopped at "Bob's Kwik Stop" for a soda. I pulled in, left my car running, and hopped out. A good-neighboring friend was mowing his lawn. When I gave him a wave to say hi, he collapsed. I ran as fast as I could to him. He was having a heart attack, but I did not know this since so many things were happening so fast. I screamed for help as loud as I could, but there was no one there.

Finally someone came out of the store. I yelled at them to go back into the store and call an ambulance. While that was going on I checked his pulse—he had one; a weak one, then it stopped. I then started CPR on his chest. I did not give him mouth to mouth because he was kind of choking, that means air is escaping. I stopped CPR, checked his pulse. It was slight, then it stopped again. I started pounding on his chest again. This is the scary part, I knew he was gone when his eyes bulged and his face turned purple. I watched a man die in my hands.

I know I did all I could do, but it still scares the hell out of me. The ambulance arrived, they worked on him for a half-hour there, giving him shock treatment and continued CPR. They packed him into the ambulance and took him to the hospital. I called my mother—she was working at the hospital. She said that he didn't make it. Although I knew he didn't make it when I was working on him I thought there was a chance at the hospital to revive him. It was just all too scary. All the courses I have taken on CPR, etc. don't really teach you until you experience it. I am still shaking on the inside. I am going to his wake tonight since he was a friend.

I work at the funeral home and I deal with the dead all the time and it doesn't bother me. Seeing this living being lose life is beyond anything I can write or say. It scares me to imagine how fast life comes and goes. I just pray to God that I have a fulfilling life and that he takes me at the right time.

Sincerely,
Jamie P.

Figure 3-5, The Writing Center Student Summer Letter

What's in a Name?

You will notice that I called our writing center staff members student-editors or editors. To a degree, these titles oppose the more traditional writing center language. Throughout the writing center world, the titles used include tutors, consultants, and writing coaches, and I'll use these various names in this book. However, I am partial to using "editor" because of the proud history and vital role editors play in the writing world. My longtime editor and dear friend, Anne Wood, has listened and listened, read and reread my work. Through e-mail, phone calls, and face-to-face conversations, Anne has gently moved my writing, and me, to new levels. She has also helped me with my crazy constructions and grammatical gaffes. Writers depend on their editors for so much—clearly, ours is a partnership. This relationship is what we want for our students.

People tend to confuse the role of "editor" with "copy editor," those persnickety wunderkinds who know all those subtle technical rules that make our writing clearer. Editors are guides, confidants, and caretakers—yes, they do make suggestions about technique and comment on conventions, but first and foremost editors and writers form relationships while talking about the ever-emerging story of a piece of writing.

Understanding Writing as a Process

In our first few sessions, my student-editors and I speak continually about writing as a process. It's the time when they discover how highly individualized and personal the writing process is. Next, we journal. "Think about a piece of your writing and write about your process from start to finish." Here's part of what Janet wrote in her journal:

> When I wrote my autobiography, I started by making lists like the people in my life:
> Friends, family, acquaintances (?), coaches, my minister, teachers who I loved,

neighbors, boyfriends. After that list I made a list of the big things that had happened in my sixteen years→ Born, kindergarten with Mrs. Ramsey, my sister Teri is born, my grandparents moved to Florida for winters, 4th grade talent show, Mr. Downs my first man teacher, trip to Disney World, summer camp and then becoming a counselor in training, met Adam in the 8th grade, high school, left Adam in 9th grade and went with Jarod, HOBY 10th grade year. You gave me some advice about this paper, Mr. Kent. You said to think about important books, movies, music, and stuff that would help show the reader who I am as a person. So I made lists of all that too. After that I kind of outlined the paper into sections into major happenings, people, major influences. Then I wrote a first draft and fixed it up myself by doing spell-check and grammar-check. My mother always goes over my writing and makes suggestions...

Once they complete the journal, I ask them to take a piece of 2' x 3' news-print and draw a map of their process. They present their writing process poster to the class. Depending on the number of students, this activity can take the entire ninety-minute class.

The student-editors' presentations reveal how our writing processes have differences and similarities:

"I just start writing," admits Ryan. "Stuff just comes to me. Then, I fix it and give it to Julie to look over. Julie knows how to help me."

"I draw idea webs like I learned with Mrs. Wheeler in 4th grade," says Cara. "Then I sketch out an outline and start writing using the outline as a guide. It's not one of those Roman numeral kind of outlines—it's simpler than that. Then, I write. I do my first revision and then ask my homeroom teacher, Mr. Carver, to look it over. He always has good suggestions."

"I make lists of ideas and then I write," says Ryan. "It works for me."

After a class discussion, we agree that the fundamental process includes, in some form or another, the following phases:

1. Prewriting and Planning
2. Drafting and Discovering
3. Revising, Editing, and Proofreading
4. Publishing or Presenting

I often supplement these discussions with short articles by writing authorities such as Donald M. Murray, Peter Elbow, Donald Graves, Thomas Newkirk, Tom Romano, and Nancie Atwell.

Prewriting or Planning: During this phase of the process, writers gather ideas. We think about our audience and consider the form our writing will take (e.g., story, letter, essay, article, or speech). Some of the strategies we use as writers (or as editors helping a writer) during this stage of the process include freewriting or a quick-write, talking with teachers, friends, or experts, webbing, making lists, or researching books, articles, or websites.

Drafting and Discovering: This phase of the process requires writing without serious concern for correctness. It's about getting ideas on paper and, often, as James Britton writes, "[to] discover what it was we meant to say" (1982, p. 20). Coupled with Britton's words, the following quotation on writing by Jacques Barzun is helpful when we're discussing first drafts:

Beginning to Write

To know how to begin to write is a great art. Convince yourself that you are working in clay, not marble; on paper, not eternal bronze; let the first sentence be as stupid as it wishes. No one will rush out and print it as it stands. Just put it down; and then another. Your whole first paragraph or first page may have to be guillotined after your piece is finished; but there can be no second paragraph until you have a first.

Revising, Editing, and Proofreading: During this step of the process, we reexamine our purpose in writing to ensure that what we set out to do has been accomplished. At this point we might share the piece with a trusted reader (e.g., writing center tutor, teacher) for feedback. The focus of this stage of the process is to look closely at the structure, content, and mechanics of the piece.

Writer-editor Brenda Miller Power passed along this quotation on revision by Naomi Shihab Nye:

...If a teacher told me to revise, I thought that meant my writing was a broken-down car that needed to go to the repair shop. I felt insulted. I didn't realize the teacher was saying, 'Make it shine. It's worth it.' Now I see revision as a beautiful word of hope. It's a new vision of something. It means you don't have to be perfect the first time. What a relief! (Personal correspondence, 2005)

Publishing or Presenting: Often, this phase of school writing is wholly incomplete. Frequently, school writing is read by or published for a one-member audience: the teacher. Sometimes, by two: a classmate and the teacher. In some cases student writing is put up—published—on a wall in the classroom. Personally, I have never been able to stand and read an entire essay taped to a wall. As writing center faculty advisors, we can help teachers realize the power of publishing as a motivating factor for our students. Encouraging this phase of the process by suggesting publishing ideas is vital. A few publishing suggestions include the following:

- Reading day: Put aside an entire class period for students to share their final products with classmates.

- Class trades: Trade final pieces with a colleague's class and ask the students to respond to each other's writing.
- Parents-caregivers: At the beginning of the year in a letter home, ask for parent-caregiver volunteers to be outside reader-responders of student work. Send kids' writing to a caring adult for feedback.
- Class book: At the end of each quarter or marking period, ask students to select a favorite piece to be included in the class book. Have the book available in multiple copies in your classroom and place a copy in the library/media center magazine rack. Spiral binding and an attractive cover will do much to grab a reader's attention.
- Class Weblog: Your class may maintain a Weblog on the Web where students may post their writing for others to review and, perhaps, comment on. You may even have a Weblog that is a partnership with another school across the country.
- School server: Publishing stories, poems, or essays on the school's website or on an e-mail site does much to promote writing and your writing center.
- Retired teachers: These folks may be willing to be readers and responders of student writing.
- District teachers: Asking your colleagues from the younger grades to read student work may sound burdensome, but often these teachers want to see what students' writing is like at the upper grades. A smiley face (☺) sticker and a few choice words of encouragement from an elementary school teacher can be just the inspiring audience a secondary student needs. You may also return the favor by reading a set of stories from your guest reader's classroom.
- Principal, assistant principal, guidance counselor, school nurse, food service, custodial staff, superintendent, curriculum coordinator, school board members: Asking any of these folks to read some or all of the stories from one class and to write a short, encouraging comment is a way to involve your entire school community with your kids' writing. Watch your students when they read what caring adults have written to them.
- College teachers and students: If you have a college of education nearby, you may find that a professor there might like some authentic essays to share with her or his students. You may also find that your university writing center colleague may welcome writing from 6th-12th graders to help train university editors.
- Community members: You may develop a cadre of community readers who are willing to take on stories to read and respond to. From

firefighters to senior citizen groups, service organizations (e.g., Rotary) to local businesses or corporations, we never know who will welcome the opportunity to be a reader of our kids' work.
- A wide variety of outlets for student writing abound, both online and not: Use any search engine to connect.

What can a writing center consultant do during the publication phase? Caring consultants may ask the student writer to bring back the final draft after the teacher assesses it. "I'd love to read your final piece—I really like this story!" This offer is incredibly motivating. Consultants won't be able to read every student's final draft, but savvy consultants can determine who needs that little bit extra to provide encouragement for the next writing assignment.

The Tutoring Process with a Draft

I ask my students, "When you share a piece of writing with a teacher or a friend—a piece that you've really worked hard on—what do you feel like?"

"My whole body gets jumpy—like, I mean, *everything*. My legs feel tingly, my face gets red, my heart...I hate it!" admits Erin, her arms waving.

"I get hyper like Erin but I also get, like, defensive," says Geny. "I think that helps me get prepared."

"I'm pumped to hear what they're going to say, but I'm also kinda scared," admits Brian.

Finally, I add my thoughts about handing over a piece of writing: "I have so many emotions about sharing my writing that I can't describe them," I say. "When I've been working on a book for a long time—you know, like for six months or more—when I hand the draft over to my editor, I sit around and wonder all sorts of stuff. Mostly, I just want to hear her say, 'Oh, Rich, you are the best writer!'"

Most students admit that having our important writing read and critiqued is a nerve-racking time. We also admit that it's a time when kindness and hope mean more than correction. We writers want to hear that our writing is okay— or has the possibility of being okay—which is to say that we are okay. A good editor knows how to sneak into your process and help you clean it up and smooth it out. Effective editors make us excited to write more. Helping student writers become effective editors often means helping them think about kindness, caring, and sensitivity.

In the movie *As Good as It Gets* with Jack Nicholson, we hear Jack's obsessive compulsive character say to a love interest, "You make me want to be a better man." It's one of my favorite movie lines. As editors, tutors, or consultants—caretakers of a writer's writing—our ultimate job is to help writers say, "You make me want to be a better writer."

Connect with the Writer

Sometimes in my writing center class, I role-play being a fat-headed, know-it-all member of the writing center staff. The student writer walks in and I grab the paper, uncap my BIG red felt pen, and start bleeding on the sucker without as much as a hello. During the skit I laugh snidely, roll my eyes, and end up staring at the writer as if he were a dust mite. My students laugh; they get the point.

As writing center personnel, we begin a tutorial or conference with personal talk beyond the paper. We connect and try to form a relationship—we're friendly and reassuring. It's this personal talk that breaks the ice and helps the writer feel comfortable to share.

Preliminary Questions

When we begin to confer about the piece, we don't take the paper away from the writer; we share it. And usually as writing center tutors we don't write on the writer's paper—that's their job, in most cases. We entice the writer into talking about the paper by asking questions such as the following:

- Who assigned the paper?
- What is the specific assignment?
- Do you have an assignment sheet that I could read?
- What points would you like to make?
- How's the paper going so far? Is there anything that you're worried about?

Read Aloud

If the writer is comfortable, she should read the paper aloud. During the reading the student-editor makes notes and listens with power. I role-play this with my students, too. Leaning back in our chairs, picking at a cuticle, or looking around the room all signal to the writer and scream: "You and your writing aren't important to me." Be supportive: Lean forward, smile, nod, chuckle, or laugh where appropriate (Don't be phony!); encourage the writer with an "Oh, that's so cool." In essence, be there wholly and honestly. After the reading—and it may have been the student-editor who read the paper aloud—ask the writer if she noticed anything while reading. Ask about changes she might want to make. If there are, discuss those issues. If the writer stares blankly, begin with an analysis by questioning.

Questions Writing Center Staffers Might Ask About a Draft:

- Has the writer addressed the teacher's assignment?
- Is the piece of writing focused and does it stay on a central idea?
- Does the piece have a beginning, middle, and an ending?
- Are these sections (i.e., beginning, middle, ending) well developed? If not, what are the weaknesses and what can be done about them?
- Is each paragraph complete? If not, what might be added?
- Do any paragraphs have multiple themes? If so, should they be divided into two paragraphs?
- Do any arguments seem weak?

Correcting Mistakes?

"But what about mistakes, Mr. Kent?" asks Karolyn, a senior editor who will in a half dozen years or so become an English teacher herself.

"First, we focus on ideas and higher-order issues," I say. "Then, we help with errors. Correcting errors first is like painting a wall before you have filled in the holes on the surface of that wall." They stare at me with their squinty-eyed, *sometimes-you-act-real-old* look. Unlike me, these teenagers don't repair the horsehair-plaster walls of a 100-year-old Victorian house as I do on many weekends.

"OK. It's like handing out the game uniforms to a football team before they have had pre-season triple sessions in August. You know, before they know the plays and have gotten into shape." My jock kids nod.

"It's like painting a car that doesn't run," I explain. "It's like frosting a burnt cake or building a beautiful home without a solid foundation or giving a concert before..."

"OK! OK! We get it," says Karolyn. "First, the basics of a paper: the ideas, the thinking, the stuff of it. Then we worry about making it pretty or correct."

"Yes!"

The second phase of the tutorial is completed, I explain, by asking general questions to see whether the writer simply made a careless mistake with commas or subject-verb agreement, or whether she doesn't understand the rules.

I explain, "Noticing a comma splice, I might say something like 'There's a punctuation problem in this sentence.' The writer looks it over and either finds it or not. If not, we might say, 'You have a comma here...' and you ask, 'Can you explain why you placed one here?'"

"You just don't tell him?" asks Shawn. He knows the answer immediately as I slowly raise my arm and point toward the sign just above the whiteboard: "Being told is the opposite of finding out." Mr. Britton always seems to have the answer.

I hope that I do a good job explaining the purpose of *coaching* writers versus *correcting* a paper. It's important to impress upon our writing center coaches that their roles are to teach, and as novice teachers they have to realize that they don't have to be perfect or have all the answers. At times, I explain, writing center tutors will have to look in a resource book such as a grammar text—we all do. When students work with students in this fashion, they are working as partners, as co-editors of a piece of writing. This collaboration helps both students discover that writing, though at times solitary, is a social affair.

What If There's No Draft?

If a student arrives in the writing center without a draft, our work as editors is to guide them through the beginning phases of the writing process. Naturally, we begin with chit-chatting in an effort to connect with the writer. Those without drafts can be frazzled, so taking the time to make them feel comfortable and reassured is important.

Next, we review the assignment from the teacher and ask the student writer how she usually proceeds with a writing project. In other words, we try to find out her process. As editors we can accomplish this by asking a series of questions similar to the following:

- Tell me about something you've written that you're proud of.
- How'd you go about writing it? What was your process?
- What aspects of your writing process are easy for you?
- What aspects of your writing process are difficult?
- What did you learn about when you wrote this paper?
- Did you learn anything about your writing process when you wrote this paper?
- What do you do differently as a result of writing this paper?

Our job as writing coaches is to honor the writer's process, and if possible, to help them refine and improve upon it. Again, in some fashion or another, the process will include the following: prewriting and planning; drafting and discovering; revising, editing, and proofreading; and publishing or presenting.

Our focus without a draft is to clarify the assignment and to make a plan. We can do this through a series of questions such as the following:

- Tell me in your own words what this assignment is about.
- What have you been thinking about as a focus? (Ask this question if there's a choice involved.)
- What else have you written in this class?
- Did you feel successful with this paper?
- When it was returned, what advice or instruction did you receive from your teacher about this paper?
- Beyond your teacher, who's your audience for this new paper? (If it's only going to be read by the teacher and not "published," perhaps leading the writer to consider other readers will help them figure out an approach. For example, if they're writing a book review, perhaps the readers could be students from another class in the school.)
- Depending on how the questioning is going, you may move on to issues in prewriting such as the following:

  ✓ What do you know about this topic?
  ✓ Would you like to make a list of ideas about the topic you've chosen?
  ✓ How about forming a web of ideas?
  ✓ Where would you research if you wanted to find out more about this topic?

Obviously, there are many questions that can be asked. The idea is to get the writer talking about the subject and playing with ideas. Together, come up with a plan of attack for the assignment and, perhaps, offer more help when they have a draft underway.

Minimalist Tutoring

"At its core," says Ryan Middleswart, a tutor in the University of Maine Writing Center, "the idea of minimalist tutoring is a simple one—minimize the dependence of a student writer on using a tutor."

A secondary English education major and my research assistant on this book, Ryan explained, "a tutor uses questions that help students identify problem areas in their work on their own and that help guide the writer to find the solutions to these problems themselves. This idea essentially takes the power out of the tutor's hands and puts this power where it belongs—in the proverbial pen of the writer."

Ryan offered several tips to help ensure that student-editors effectively use the minimalist tutoring strategy:

- Don't be in a hurry to jump into a writer's paper. Taking a few minutes to get to know the student, assignment, and concerns about their writing will help to make the student feel more at ease about handing their private thoughts over to a stranger.
- Try to sit in a way that makes the editor and student equals, such as sitting next to each other. Avoid the "boss/employee" style of sitting across from each other, for this not only makes looking at a paper together difficult, but also breeds a more hierarchical feel.
- If the student is willing, have her read the paper out loud to the editor. Reading aloud will help let the editor listen for problem areas while keeping the work in the writer's hands. Also, it is incredible how many mistakes the writer catches as he reads aloud.
- Try to refrain from writing on the paper or taking the paper out of the student's hands. Remember, it is their work and their words, and tutors are only there to guide the writer in the right direction.
- While most student writers react best to minimalist tutoring, others warrant a more directive approach and will balk at answering questions. So while the minimalist approach is preferable in helping to guide a student writer in the right direction, neither approach is necessarily right or wrong. Try to use your instincts in deciding which strategy to utilize.

For more information about minimalist tutoring, read the section from *The St. Martin's Sourcebook for Writing Tutors* (2003) by Jeff Brooks, "Minimalist Tutoring: Making the Student Do All the Work" (pp. 83-87). In addition, you will find numerous statements about minimalist tutoring on writing center websites. Check out the webpage below from the Livingston Writing Center—Rutgers, The State University of New Jersey, titled "Minimalist Tutoring." Such disclaimers will help writers further understand the role of their student-editors.

Minimalist Tutoring

Students receive individualized and directed assistance to develop their reading and writing skills. The primary goal of the center is to move students towards independence in these skills. The tutor will help you learn to read closely, develop critical readings, revise your drafts, and correct your errors on your own.

The tutor will not do the work for you, correct your paper, or act as a proofreader or style-checker. Rather the tutor will work with you on your own paper to help you learn how to revise, complicate, and develop your own readings of texts. The tutor will also work with you to develop the skills necessary to determine and correct your own patterns of error.

This approach to tutoring is minimalist in that it seeks to minimize your dependence upon the writing tutor. The tutor's job is to assist you in identifying problem areas with your writing, to provide you with a concrete plan for working on those areas, to allow you the time to begin doing that work yourself, and to provide you with guidance when you get stuck.

© Livingston Writing Center—Rutgers, The State University of New Jersey

Online Tutoring or Virtual Peer Review

Many OWLs (Online Writing Labs) offer online tutoring or editing services. When I write "editing services," I mean written feedback about a piece of writing not corrections. Teaching our students to provide thoughtful guidance and feedback in written form is a challenge. Different writing center directors have different guidelines for training their personnel with online tutoring. What is more, some OWLs offer real time chat room tutoring. The dialog between writer and editor can be carried on via e-mail, instant messaging, iSight, fax, or even over free Internet telephone companies like Skype (www.skype.com). Our 21st century teenagers thrive on IM and e-mailing. If this use of technology is intimidating to you, let the students teach you the many ways we might use technology to support writing!

As mentioned earlier, the Claremont Graduate University Writing Center staff offers online consulting via e-mail (www.cgu.edu/pages/782.asp). The service is available every day of the academic year for Claremont Graduate University students and staff. Once a paper is submitted, it is sent on to a writing center consultant who will read the paper and return it with comments. The turnaround time for comments is astounding: Papers up to fifteen double-spaced pages: approximately forty-eight hours. Papers from sixteen to fifty double-spaced pages: approximately seven days. The Online Consultants do read and comment on papers over fifty pages long; however, if it's the chapter of a dissertation or the like, they do encourage writers to submit the piece in sections.

To submit a paper to the Claremont Writing Center Online, students must include basic information such as address and e-mail. They must also respond to the following:

- Word processing program and version you use (this may affect the format in which consultants provide comments to you)
- Course for which you're writing the paper

- How you heard about the writing center
- Your particular concerns about the paper
- A description of the assignment and any criteria the professor has for the paper
- A list of questions for the consultant or a statement of your concerns about the draft

A series of books, or sections from books, will support a director in developing online tutoring. Those books include but are not limited to the following:

Breuch, Lee-Ann Kastman. (2004). *Virtual Peer Review: Teaching and Learning about Writing in Online Environments.* Albany, NY: SUNY Press.

Inman, James A. and Sewell, Donna M. (2000). *Taking Flight with OWLs: Examining Electronic Writing Center Work.* Mahwah, NJ: Lawrence Erlbaum.

Inman, James A. and Gardner, C. (2001). *The OWL Construction and Maintenance Guide.* Emmitsburg, MA: IWCA Press.

Hobson, Eric H. (1998). *Wiring the Writing Center.* Logan, UT. Utah University Press.

Gillespie, Paula and Lerner, Neal. (2004). *The Allyn and Bacon Guide to Peer Tutoring.* 2nd ed. Upper Saddle River, NJ: Longman.

Rafoth, Ben. (Ed.). (2005). *A Tutor's Guide: Helping Writers One to One.* 2nd ed. Portsmouth, NH: Heinemann–Boynton/Cook.

McAndrew, D. A. and Reigstad, T. J. (2001). *Tutoring Writing: A Practical Guide for Conferences.* Portsmouth, NH: Heinemann–Boynton/Cook.

Conferring online via e-mail or instant messaging (IM) versus face-to-face (f2f) remains a discussion piece among post-secondary writing center directors. One particular discussion took place on the "Writing Center Mailing List" (March 1, 2005) where Roberta Kjesrud, the Writing Center Coordinator at Western Washington University, commented in a thoughtful and forward-thinking fashion:

E-mail tutoring has grown to about thirty percent of our business at the moment. We wouldn't have predicted it when we initiated this service a few years ago, but when we were moved to an attic of the library a couple of years ago, the new location just didn't draw students. Fortunately, online conferencing is completely portable, and it's been "discovered" by our students in a big way. Although many use f2f conferencing as the gold standard for what conferencing should be, we've been grateful for the opportunity to discover that e-mail conferencing has extremely important outcomes.

As a staff, we've come to appreciate that online conferencing can't be thought of as worse than—prevailing attitude seems to be "it will do in a pinch." Rather, online conferencing has unique benefits to both writers and responders. Responders appreciate the chance to be more thoughtful and deliberate in agenda setting and in word choice. They like the extra time to consider priorities, select them with deliberation, and sign-post those choices to writers. Writers appreciate the convenience—they can contact us at their point of need and then forget it for a while. They also like the anonymity—many are intimidated to share their writing (I know I am!). But mostly, they *love* having written responses that they can refer to over and over as they revise. Our experience matches the research that shows writers demonstrate more ownership of and agency in revising choices when they receive written peer review. Also, we're very surprised by the number of writers who voluntarily get back to us after they get our e-mails—much more so than in f2f work. I've come to realize that it's very hard to say "OWLing doesn't work." Just as in f2f teaching, pedagogy is everything. We pay special attention to make sure our online pedagogy reflects the values we hold in f2f conferences and in teaching and learning in general. As distance education has already demonstrated, the online medium works very well for teaching and learning. HOW you teach and learn online makes all the difference. (Kjesrud, 2005)

Some folks might question whether 6th-12th grade students are seasoned enough to respond to writers in this fashion. My answer is, "Why not?" Helping your students learn to write responses to other students' writing will help them realize even more how tough writing and editing is. In addition, such work will help them focus in on specifics. Writing in response to writing is a class assignment used to promote lots of useful conversation about writing, revision, and response.

Working with Diverse Populations

Your student-editors will work with a wide variety of populations such as nonnative speakers of English (NNS), students with special needs, faculty, staff, and community members. Each writer who walks into your writing center arrives with a unique set of needs. Perhaps an exchange student from Slovakia will walk through the doors with a relatively sophisticated knowledge of written English but an inability to speak English well enough to communicate his needs. On the other hand, a student with special learning needs may be extraordinarily articulate but lacking in writing and reading skills. (It's not uncommon for students with special needs to compensate for literacy tangles by sharpening their verbal skills.) My student-editors' experiences with adult clients were almost always brilliant. I'm remembering our golf-crazed principal asking a staff member to review a piece he had written for a state golf magazine. The two had a blast talking sports and the article. A school board member came by with a piece of fiction he had written—a long conversation ensued.

I hadn't done any specific training about diverse populations with my student-editors. I just asked them to follow the basic rules of our writing center: Be kind, welcoming, and encouraging—and dump the red pen. Consequently, we waded our ways through a variety of editing situations with classroom conversations about the challenges. In retrospect, I now know that I could have had these conversations in advance to prepare my students for a variety of encounters. It just never occurred to me during the first couple of years of our writing center's existence. Now, I know I would bring in our district's teacher of ESL to offer a workshop; I would also invite in a teacher from the special needs department to explain learning styles and learning differences.

Many books, articles, and websites about working with ESL students offer important insight. Bruce and Rafoth's *ESL Writers: A Guide for Writing Center Tutors* (2004) presents a wide-ranging series of articles that will help in creating a curriculum for student-editors. Focused more for the collegiate level, *ESL Writers* will nonetheless provide a solid foundation for 6th-12th grade staff. In an e-mail exchange, Ben Rafoth recommended the following chapters from *ESL Writers* for 6th-12th grade student-editors and their faculty-directors:

Chapter 3: "Getting Started" by Shanti Bruce

Chapter 4: "Reading an ESL Writer's Text" by Paul Kei Matsuda and Michelle Cox

Chapter 6: "'Earth Aches by Midnight': Helping ESL Writers Clarify Their Intended Meaning" by Amy Jo Minett

Chapter 8: "Editing Line by Line" by Cynthia Linville

Chapter 15: "ESL Students Share their Writing Center Experiences" by Shanti Bruce

Gillespie and Lerner's *The Allyn and Bacon Guide to Peer Tutoring*, 2nd edition (2004), includes a helpful chapter titled "Working with ESL Writers" (p. 117). In this chapter, the authors explore eight myths about working with ESL or nonnative speakers. Gillespie and Lerner use the term "nonnative English speaker" because many of their college-level students "have English as a third or fourth language or grew up in bilingual (or trilingual) households" (p. 117).

Eight Myths of Working with NNS:

- NNS Writers have weak command of standard written English.

- NNS writers think differently from native English speakers.
- NNS writers come to the writing center to get their grammar checked.
- NNS writers just need more of the basics before they can move on to more substantial writing tasks.
- I need to clean up the grammar in NNS writers' papers before we can get to higher-order concerns.
- I need to be well-versed in the terminology of English grammar and usage if I'm to tutor NNS writers.
- So much of the English language is idiomatic and thus can never be taught.
- I'll need to be a much more directive tutor with NNS writers.

The Writing Lab at Purdue University has a thorough webpage, "ESL Resources for Students," replete with a host of links. It's a great study site for your writing center staff.

Explore these various resources, but also ask student-editors what kinds of problems they believe NNS/ESL students will encounter with writing. Talk about the issues that surface and discuss the various approaches they may use toward solutions. Then, seek further information from authoritative sources by sharing a variety of readings on ESL students and writing. Most important of all: With 6th-12th grade student-editors we must emphasize the social aspect of talking about a piece of writing with NNS/ESL students. An editorial session between two teenagers from different countries has to be fun as well as educational.

Ask your foreign language or ESL teachers to come speak with your staff about learning a second language in schools today. These teachers will talk about playful activities such as skits and the power of laughter to encourage second language learners to be adventurous with the language. Many of us learn a second language most effectively through immersion. Indeed, NNS/ESL students must be allowed and encouraged to experiment and play with the language. Remind your student-editors: Don't be a corrector first with ESL students—or with anyone for that matter.

Kids with learning differences come with a unique set of issues, not the least of which is a lack of self-esteem. As with the ESL approach, have student-editors talk about issues that they believe face kids with learning differences. Next, pass out "During Christmas vacation and The other Vacation's" from "Peter's Story: Another Way of Seeing" (Kent, 1997, pp. 44-50). A former student, "Peter" lives with fetal alcohol syndrome (FAS). Have your students read his one-page, single-spaced Christmas story and outline what they see as strong writing. The following is a small sample of Peter's writing:

> During Christmas vacation and The other Vacation's. On Christmas eve morning me and my dad went up in the woods to go make a couple of hitches. When we got there we tried to start up the skitter after a while we got it started we put the chokechains on the back of the skitter. After I got done putting the chokechains on I put my chap's on and got onto the skitter and went to go get a hitch of tree's. When my dad cut's down the tree's I have to hitch them up and if I feel like I limb the tree's sometimes. Around 12:00 we ate lunch and headed back up to get more hitches of wood when we went back down to the yard the pulp truck was there so I unhooked the log's and went to park the skitter.

Ask the students to gather in small groups of three or four to share their thinking about the strengths of the piece. Finally, have the students discuss the conversation they might have with Peter about his writing. In "Peter's Story: Another Way of Seeing" there is a letter by me focused on the strengths of the boy's writing. I've written the letter to his special needs teacher. After you lead your students through this activity, you might wish to share my letter for further discussion.

For more information consult the ERIC website "Information Center on Disabilities and Gifted Education" (http://ericec.org). To find useful articles search the Web using the following: "Teaching Writing Skills to Students with Disabilities." My friend and special education colleague, Dr. Diane Jackson, also recommends the website LD Online (www.ldonline.org) and a specific writing site for the writing needs of kids with learning difficulties (www.ldonline.org/ld_indepth/writing/writing.html).

Finally, speak to those exemplars of education, your colleagues in the special needs department. Most will be thrilled to come and speak with your writing center students about working with kids who learning differently.

Recommended Reading for Writing Center Staff

Clearly, what I have provided above is a glimpse. The following online handbooks, websites, and mail lists may be quite helpful for your writing center staffers and your school colleagues. Many writing centers and OWLs have how-to handbooks posted and available for downloading on their websites. These guides offer practical, uncomplicated information for writing center staff members. And as always, for updated information, stay connected to www.writingcenters.org (the International Writing Centers Association website).

Peer Tutor Handbooks Online:

Tufts University:
http://ase.tufts.edu/wts-writingfellows/handbook/main.asp

Penn State:
http://www.psu.edu/dept/cew/writingcenter/handbook.htm

Tutor.edu: a Manual for Writing Center Tutors:
http://www.montreat.edu/tutor

Colorado State University:
http://writing.colostate.edu/wcenter/wchandbook.htm

University of South Carolina, Aiken:
http://www.usca.edu/writingroom/manual.html

Washburn University:
http://www.wuacc.edu/services/zzcwwctr/handbook3.txt

University of Houston:
http://www.uh.edu/writecen/consultants/WritingConsultantHandbook.pdf

University of Detroit, Mercy:
http://liberalarts.udmercy.edu/%7Ericeje/wcenter/handbook

University of North Carolina at Chapel Hill:
http://www.unc.edu/depts/wcweb/staff_manual.html

Online Websites and Mail Lists:

The Dangling Modifier
This website features the newsletter for peer tutors and includes a collection of past issues from which you may glean articles of specific interest to your student-editors and you.
http://www.ulc.psu.edu/Dangling_Modifier

Friends of Writing Center Journal Blog
This blog features writing by authors whose work has appeared in the IWCA's *The Writing Center Journal*. As with most blogs, responses are posted by many folks, most of whom are writing center directors and student-editors.
http://writingcenterjournal.blogspot.com

Peer Centered
This blog is for writing tutors, consultants, and student-editors from around the world. As the Peer Centered's information states, "Since many writing

centers already keep their own shared, we think this is a good way to promote/explore writing center work. Bloggers here will share their ideas, experiences, or insight." Though currently focused on post-secondary writing centers, 6th-12th grade student-editors and their submissions would be welcomed.
http://bessie.englab.slcc.edu/pc

Writing Lab Newsletter Online
Back issues of Purdue's *Writing Lab Newsletter* may be accessed via their website. There is a searchable database for back issues; Adobe Portable Document Format (PDF) is necessary for viewing and printing.
Search: Index of *Writing Lab Newsletter* Volumes
http://owl.english.purdue.edu/lab/newsletter/

Praxis: A Writing Center Journal
An online journal based at the University of Texas at Austin's Undergraduate Writing Center, *Praxis* includes articles written by tutors and writing center directors concerning issues such as training, consulting strategies, and professional development.
http://uwc3.fac.utexas.edu/~praxis/

International Writing Centers Association Discussion Forum
An online forum that may be found on the IWCA website.
http://www.writingcenters.org/board/index.php

WCenter
An online discussion forum for writing center directors and tutors from which you may receive e-mail.
http://lyris.acs.ttu.edu/cgi-bin/lyris.pl?join=wcenter

Secondary School Writing Center Listserv (SSWC-L)
A mailing list for secondary school writing center directors. Information on this list may be found on the International Writing Centers Association webpage. At this writing, interested secondary school writing center directors or would-be directors may subscribe to SSWC-L by sending an e-mail to LISTSERV@LISTS.PSU.EDU with "subscribe SSWC-L your name" in the body of the message.

Cal Berkeley Student Learning Center Writing Program
http://slc.berkeley.edu

Stanford University Writing Center
http://swc.stanford.edu

National Conference on Peer Tutoring in Writing (NCPTW)
http://www.wc.iup.edu/ncptw

University of Richmond's Training for Tough Tutorials
These video training clips and tutorials could be helpful for your student-editors to view. Most of all these videos will help raise discussion points. You must have a fast connection to view these videos.
http://writing2.richmond.edu/training/tough/index.html

The Writery: Massey University in New Zealand
The Writery has an interactive grammar site that offers lessons and quizzes. This site might be a good one for your student-editors and for their clients. In fact, it could be a good one for them to do together if the writer has challenges with conventions.
http://writery.massey.ac.nz/ramosus_list.asp

The Writery's online community is extensive and they invite you to join in the Writers' Zone (http://writery.massey.ac.nz/studyhome.asp). The Writers' Zone offers other interactive features, including the Writing Café. Here, writers post work for feedback and critique another's work. Discussions occur on all aspects of writing and real time discussions take place in the site's chat rooms. According to the site, The Writery also offers "light-hearted competitions, prompts to get you writing when you're blocked, and resources of interest to all writers." You must register to join the website, but it's free.

Suggested Books for Writing Center Staff and Directors

The books I list could be a part of your writing center library. If you have a separate class for writing center students, select one of these books as a class text. The conversations that surface will help your students become more effective student-editors. The following books focus on college writing center tutors. However, most sections will be helpful for 6th-12th grade student-editors:

Working with Student Writers: Essays on Tutoring and Teaching
Podis, L. and Podis, J., eds. (1999). New York: Peter Lang.
*This book offers practical advice written by peer tutors.

A Tutor's Guide: Helping Writers One to One
Rafoth, B., ed. (2000). Portsmouth, NH: Heinemann.
*Presents typical problems faced by peer tutors; offers models and approaches.

Tutoring Writing: A Practical Guide for Conferences
McAndrew, Donald A. and Reigstad, Thomas J. (2001). Portsmouth, NH: Boyton/Cook.
*A full range of practical suggestions for the peer tutors, from tutoring models to dealing with writers with unique problems.

The St. Martin's Sourcebook for Writing Tutors, 2nd edition
Murphy, C. and Sherwood, S., eds. (2003). New York: St. Martin's Press.
*Current ideas about tutoring, scholarly essays, and FAQs on being a peer tutor.

A Short Course in Writing, 4th edition
Bruffee, Kenneth A. (1997). Boston: Longman.
*With an emphasis on collaborative learning throughout, this book helps students write position papers, exploring, explaining, or defending ideas they develop on topics of their own choosing. Over fifty classroom-tested collaborative exercises are included....

The Bedford Guide for Writing Tutors, 3rd edition
Ryan, Leigh. (2002). Boston: Bedford.
*A brief guide with strategies and suggestions for writing center staffers.

The Allyn and Bacon Guide to Peer Tutoring, 2nd edition
Gillespie, P. and Lerner, N. (2004). Boston: Longman.
*A comprehensive guide to effective tutoring.

Publications of Interest to Writing Center Faculty-Directors and Advanced Students:

Weaving Knowledge Together: Writing Centers and Collaboration
Haviland, C. and Wolf, T. (1998). Emmitsburg, MA: NWCA Press.
*Exploring the deep collaborations of writing center directors, student-editors, and student-writers.

Writing Center Resource Manual
Silk, B., ed. (1998). Emmitsburg, MA: IWCA Press.

*Practical advice and useful resources for writing center directors.

The Politics of Writing Centers
Nelson, J. and Evertz, K., eds. (2001). Portsmouth, NH: Boynton/Cook.
*Mentioned earlier, this book is an exploration of the territories of power in and beyond writing centers. These are helpful conversations for the writing center director.

Stories from the Center: Connecting Narrative and Theory in the Writing Center
Briggs L.C. and Woodbright, M., eds. (2000). Urbana, IL: NCTE.
*These narratives help writing center directors and their student-editors explore the realities of life in a writing center.

The Allyn and Bacon Guide to Writing Center Theory and Practice
Barnett, R. and Blumner, J., eds. (2001). Boston: Allyn and Bacon.
*This collection of essays and articles offers interesting insights on writing center issues including history, theory, the connection of theory and practice, diversity, technology, writing across the curriculum, the process of tutoring, and administration.

The High School Writing Center: Establishing and Maintaining One
Farrell, Pamela B. Urbana, IL: NCTE, 1989.
*Helpful essays on a variety of aspects of secondary writing centers.

"Writing Centers Research Project" at The University of Louisville

This website offers survey results and information for connecting to different sources. It also helps new members of the writing center community to see the scope of the writing center movement:

> Help preserve the history of writing centers.... The Writing Centers Research Project at the University of Louisville has established an archive–spoken memories and written records of writing center history–to preserve writing center history and facilitate scholars' research. The WCRP has begun interviewing those instrumental in creating and directing early writing centers, as well as those active in regional and national organizations and in early publications on writing centers.

You may find the website at http://coldfusion.louisville.edu/webs/a-s/wcrp/ or by writing to Writing Centers Research Project, 312 Ekstrom Library, University of Louisville, Louisville, KY 40292.

Writing a Mission Statement

Writing a mission statement for your writing center is a tough assignment. You, your student-staff, and interested English department colleagues should discuss developing a mission statement. In the years following, student-staff should read it, discuss it, and write about it. And because writing centers evolve, you may have to revise your mission statement.

Begin your journey by defining what a mission statement is. I've heard business people say that a mission statement is a cross between a slogan and an executive summary. Follow these basic steps:

- All members of the writing center community should be involved in developing the statement.
- Your writing center mission statement should say who you are, what you do, what you believe in, and why you do what you do.
- An effective mission statement is three to four sentences long and read in thirty seconds or less.
- Read, critique, and discuss other writing center mission statements as a part of your process.
- All writing center community members should approve the mission statement.

Here are two writing center mission statements—you may gather other mission statements through your favorite search engine:

Write in the Corner, Kettle Moraine High School, Wales, WI

Our goal is to enhance a cross-curriculum/whole school approach to writing-as-a-process, writing-to-learn, and writing-for-publication. Write in the Corner consultants help all writers identify, understand, and refine their personal writing process. Write in the Corner consultants offer questions in place of corrections, support instead of criticism, and understanding rather than evaluation.

Ohio State University, Mansfield, OH

The Writing Center provides free, one-on-one tutoring to all members of the Ohio State University community: students, faculty, and staff. We work with writers from all levels of experience, ability, and expertise, and we can read and respond to texts written for any course of study.

Our goal is to help students and others become better writers. Toward that end, writing center tutors emphasize writing as a process. They help writers come up with and organize ideas, then plan, draft, revise, and edit their essays and reports. Since writing is a rhetorical act, tutors also help writers craft their work to fit their audience and purpose.

Creating a Writing Center Staff Handbook

A helpful, ongoing assignment for writing center students is to develop their own handbook. This guide will be used as a class text or for workshops conducted for tutors. The key is to have student-editors involved in developing or revising this handbook. The conversations around what should be included in such a publication will be a powerful way to discuss writing, the student-editor's role, and the writing center.

The handbook can be passed along from one year to the next, and each new cadre of student-editors could be responsible for updating the volume. In addition, depending on what's included, the handbook might be of value to classroom teachers.

For further guidance, refer to the online peer tutor handbooks mentioned earlier in this chapter. You may also wish to review secondary school writing center handbooks found online. A basic staff handbook might include the following sections (and don't forget a cool cover!):

I.   Table of Contents
II. Introduction
        Includes short letters from both the faculty director
        and student directors
III. Mission Statement
IV. Job Description
        Philosophy of tutoring
            General approaches:
            With draft
            Without draft
            Online tutoring
            Writing center forms
V.   Training handouts, activities, and worksheets

A Day with a Writer

In the late fall of our first year, twelve student-editors spent a school day with the writer Monica Wood (www.monicawood.com). I approached our principal, Tom Rowe, with the idea. His "Go for it" brought about a very special day. We met at my home, and Monica led the students through a variety of writing exercises to strengthen their own understanding of the writing process, to get a sense of their voices, and to play with writing.

Part work, part celebration, the day with Monica helped these students get a broader sense of the struggles of a professional writer and an awareness of the individualized nature of each writer's process. We also downed pizza and went for a long walk. Monica ended the day by singing a stunning version of "From a Distance," a song composed by Julie Gold and often sung by Bette Midler. Monica loved the day and responded to all of us with this letter:

11/13/90
Dear Rich...and Matt, Matt, Kathy, Amy, Amy, Janet, Scott, Mike, Jamie, Craig, Chris, Erin, and Dave:

Thank you so much for inviting me to spend a day with you. I enjoyed your company so much, and was pleased beyond words with your willingness to write and share your writing, your kindness toward each other, your humor, your insights, and your passion for talking about things that matter. Sometimes I despair for the next generation, but being with you for a day restored my optimism. It was a deep pleasure to spend a few hours with people who think.

I know that a few of you are ready to embark on the evil journey that (we hope) ends up with college admission. After the essay I read, you might be tempted to dream up some alter-ego that has climbed Mount Everest or won a couple of Pulitzers, but my guess is that success will come by being exactly who you are.

Good luck and thanks again.
Sincerely, Monica Wood

A Day in a College Writing Center

This same group of student-editors spent the day at the University of Maine at Farmington's Writing Center. The events of this day helped our students connect with the professional atmosphere of a collegiate center and helped them see the potential of a job at college if they moved on to the post-secondary level.

Center director Doug Rawlins spent some of the morning talking about the operations of their center and the role of writing center tutors. Longtime friend and UMF instructor Burt deFrees spoke with the high school students about nurturing the writer through a tutorial session. As I wrote to our principal when requesting this field trip, "[Burt deFrees's talk] will go a long way in having students accept The Center as a positive place, not one of criticism."

These special days together with my student colleagues changed me as a teacher. My students and I formed deeper relationships, trusted one another more completely, and grew as classmates and as writing center staff. I wish such experiences to all writing center directors and teachers.

FAQs

How does confidentiality work within the writing center?
Our student-editors are guided by common sense. If a writer sounds as if she is going to do harm to herself or another, staff must go to their supervisor. If a student-editor suspects plagiarism, she may raise the issue with the writer. If students admit that they "borrowed" some phrases, that's an opening to help. Some students struggle with the differences between plagiarism, paraphrasing, and patchwriting (Howard, 1993); however, the final say about going to a teacher should rest in the hands of the faculty-director. Needless to say, if a writer admits to a learning difference, medical problem, or private family matter (e.g., my mother is an alcoholic), student-editors should respect the writer's privacy and not discuss these issues. It makes sense that student-editors feel free to speak about such troubling issues with the faculty-director or in staff meetings; however, again, the names of students should not be revealed.

All issues of privacy or confidentiality should be guided by common sense. Whenever a student-editor is in doubt, there's always a faculty-director ready to listen.

What if a tutor is not pulling his weight or is disrespectful or has a major weakness with language–can you let them go?
In the schools, life is about learning. We do all that we can to assist a willing novice editor improve his or her technique. Apprenticing with and observing a competent editor can be very helpful. Specific conversations with the director can assist an unskilled student-editor to improve.

What requirements are needed for an effective writing center staff?
Teaching and learning, writing and editing are at the same time mystical and grounded. Effective writing center staff are listeners and thoughtful responders; they are knowledgeable language lovers who avoid any label remotely associated with that of a corrector. The most effective writing center staff, I've found, are understated and they listen, listen, and listen. They live and dance in Vygotsky's (1978) elusive "zone of proximal development."

Any advice for teachers about addressing issues of plagiarism?
When I do inservice work on portfolios focused on my book *Room 109: The Promise of a Portfolio Classroom* (1997), teachers frequently ask how I prevent plagiarism. After all, each nine weeks I was collecting up to 120 portfolios, each with five, one-thousand-word papers, forty-eight journal entries of 150 words each, book projects, reflections, and more. My first words to teachers usually are, "Most plagiarism seems to be an instructional issue." When our

students are not treated individually and the teacher has not attempted to develop classroom relationships, when the classroom work nearly always has a singular audience (the teacher) and the student has little or no choice in subjects or themes of assignments, when the response to a piece of student work is a number grade and devoid of substantive conversation or response, some students *tend* to be less invested in their school work. (Go figure.) This tendency, I believe, can lead to plagiarism. So what do I do?

I begin the academic year with a personal letter (see Figure 3-7) in response to each student's first writing, an autobiography that is a first draft, spell-checked-only piece. Responding personally to my students' "life stories," even with a paragraph or two, shows them that I'm in this class for real and that I care. (You'll notice in Figure 3-7 that I wrote a lot more than a paragraph or two.) When I began this practice of responding personally to 100–120 Life Stories, I wrote only a paragraph or two. But with practice and by fully utilizing my three-day Labor Day holiday, I became good at responding in depth.) What's fun about this practice is that I encouraged, but did not require, my student colleagues to write back. Most did (see Figure 3-8).

Another helpful piece is that I have kids write journals on a daily basis. This way I come to know their voices and them as people. This helps me form a relationship with my student colleagues. And in my quarterly portfolio letters back to them, I comment on one or two of their personal journal entries.

In addition, I create an audience or readership beyond me for student portfolios (Figure 3-9). A classmate, a writing center student-editor, a parent/caregiver or another important adult, the student author (in a letter reflection), and the teacher (me) all write letters in response to the portfolio.

Saturday, August 30

Dear Sal,

I'm pleased that you've taken the chance and joined 109. I know the risks involved with this class. You've got an added burden knowing that Anthony was here and that he and I are friends. The thing is, Sal, I would never compare you to Anthony. I had three older siblings and a younger one, so I know how it feels to be compared. Trust me, Sal, I will get to know you. Welcome.

Your thinking about money and the impact on your family is intriguing. It's so interesting to look at the impact issues such as money have on our lives. We have the same experience when it comes to family and money. The most my dad made as a semi-skilled paper mill worker here in town was around $5,000 a year. I suppose that wasn't bad in the 1960s, but it wasn't great for a family of seven. So, you and I share a little bit of history, in a way.

I like the rhythm of your writing and the balance of sentence variety. Also, I can hear your voice in your writing. This is an awesome sign for a writer. You do have a great voice. Most of the time you use a variety of sentence structures—this makes for wonderful writing to read. And to think, this is a first draft piece. When editing, listen to your writing and make sure it sings with variety and difference.

Competing with Anthony (like I competed with my brother, Rob, who is almost two years younger than I am) is a paper in the making, isn't it? How did this competition help you grow? Did it cause any problems? How have you grown within this relationship throughout the years? How does your relationship with Anthony differ from the relationships you have with your other brothers? There's so much to your story that can be explored—take the chance.

What a great line: "I love the complicated simplicity of [baseball]." Another paper waiting to be explored! Interestingly, I know exactly what you mean by this statement. Trying to explain the subtlety of baseball to people from other countries is incredibly difficult: bottom of the 9th inning down by three, two outs, three and two on the batter, two on...sheesh, is this another paper idea?

Your love of science will take you far. I can't exactly see you in a lab coat with little round spectacles, but hey, if that's your dream, it's your dream! I do admire your wish to make a difference in our world through your work as a scientist. And if you happened to end up a biology teacher? The profession would be well served.

Well, enough for now. Sal, it's good to have you here. I hope your journey in Room 109 will be filled with risks and adventure. Be well. Pax.

YLET,
Rich Kent

Figure 3-7, Teacher's Letter Response to Life Story

Dear Mr. Kent,

It's good to know that we have something in common when it comes to our childhood. As a child my dad worked as a welder for many corporations. Welders don't get paid that much. I had the funniest looking house. One day I got bored and measured it in length and it was only twenty-five feet long on the inside, which meant it was probably thirty feet on the outside.

I don't think you will have to worry about getting me and my brother mixed up at all. We are totally different people in our writing and our personalities. He's always off in the clouds with some dream of his and I'm always the practical one. At home if my parents ever needed anything done they asked me because they knew that he wouldn't do it.

I'm really excited for Friday. It is the day of our first football game. I think it's stupid that every sport has games on the same night. I'm sure some people would like to watch some other sports. I enjoy watching soccer games and I won't be able to until late November. Even if they schedule every sport on the same night they should at least have one of the games home. That's just my thought. Good luck in your game on Friday. I will write you later.

Sincerely,
Salvatore

Figure 3-8, Student Response Letter

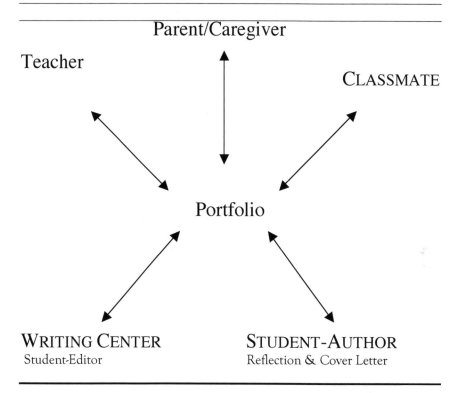

Figure 3-9, Room 109 Portfolio Response System

CHAPTER FOUR

Operating a Writing Center

Finding a Home

We began our writing center in my small classroom with four computers, one daisy-wheel printer, an endless supply of paper, and one editor for a few periods a day. The next year we had our own room across the hallway from my classroom. In our seventh year, we ended up in the media center/library, the perfect place in our school.

Where will you house your writing center? You have many options to explore, including a media center, an underutilized book or storage room, a computer lab, one or more English classrooms, study halls, the learning assistance center, the cafeteria study hall, a conference room beside the principal's office, the nurse's office (if used only certain days or hours a week), a conference room beside the guidance or student service area.... You might like to explore the options with your head custodian. You may be surprised what suggestions he or she has.

My best advice is not to worry about finding a perfect space. Just start! If you use a table in your classroom with one editor available, so be it. If you have a room and your English/language arts colleagues agree to monitor it a few periods a day, get going! If you're given a huge classroom replete with twenty-five computers, two or three teacher desks, sofas, tables, a refrigerator, flowers, paintings, a wall full of resource books, and a paid, full-time writing center professional.... Call me.

Public Relations and Marketing

I suppose the most important aspect of PR and marketing your writing center is convincing your colleagues that it's a helpful place for their students to go. We do that, as discussed in chapter two, by teaching folks in your school about the value of such a center. Your English colleagues are the primary group to convince. Hopefully, they're on board. However, even if a member is shaky about having their students use the writing center, my guess is that you'll be able to persuade any skeptics to require their students to use the writing center's services for just one paper per semester. After all, if students move on to post-secondary schooling, they will want to know how to use a writing center's services. With each student bringing in one paper per semester, your center will be busy. (When I taught 110–120 students and required a writing center tutorial on the five papers for the quarter, our student-editors were busy.)

Meeting with each department to discuss the writing center's services is a good way to begin the school-wide dialogue and marketing "campaign." Hearing your colleagues' questions and concerns will allow you to develop approaches to assuage their uncertainties and fears. These meetings can be much like those you organized with your own department and principal. Keep your presentation short, perhaps ten minutes, and allow time for conversation. Bring your laptop and projector to show an OWL from a respected college. Your request could be as simple as the following: "If you require each student to bring in one writing assignment per semester for a conference, they will have a unique experience and our writing center will be extremely busy."

"But what if the editors are poor?"

"Well, they can't get better without practice. And since some of our students are heading off to college, they'll want the experience of utilizing a writing center and deciding whether the writing center editor has made good suggestions. In the end, a writing center conference allows the writer to make decisions about her paper with someone who is there to help."

"But I don't want anyone working with my students but me."

"I do understand this. But if we are preparing our students to survive in the world beyond school, they need to have the experience of working with people other than their teachers. This experience allows them to negotiate with someone other than a paid professional and make decisions."

"I still don't like the idea."

"I do understand your concerns, but let me ask you, will one thirty- to sixty-minute session per semester over one writing assignment really harm your students? Or might the experience give them an important opportunity to discuss writing with someone else?"

Teaching your colleagues about the writing center services could mean sending out informational flyers like the one I supplied in Chapter One called "Eight Ways to Use The Writing Center" (pp. 8-9). Such handouts helped my colleagues come to understand how they can connect their classroom with the writing center.

Just like any business, your writing center needs to have an identifiable image and that image has to be displayed. In addition, association with the image has to be positive. Near the beginning of my professional career, I worked as the public relations director for a large ski resort in Maine. There, I learned that style and image have to be valued and nurtured. When you begin discussing publicity for your writing center, think about including the following:

- Logo: Create a smart-looking logo. Your students have access to great computer programs and your school will have technology experts who can help you design stellar logos. To get a sense of different logos, search the webpages of a variety of writing centers. Make the decision of selecting a logo a writing center community affair. Our first logo was an antique typewriter.
- Informational brochure: Once again, with today's technology brochures can be professionally produced. Think about the copy, layout, and potential photographs. The brochure of *Write in the Corner* at Kettle Moraine High School is a terrific model (see Figure 5-2). Also, checkout The Writing Center at University of Notre Dame brochure in Appendix C courtesy of John Duffy and Connie Mack, director and assistant director of The Writing Irish!
- Hallway Passes: Printing and publishing hallway passes (see Figure 4-1, with thanks to ideas from Monica Wood!) with your writing center's logo is one more way to showcase your center. These passes may include tips for writers, quotations by literary figures, writing from local students or staff members, or photos.
- Calendars: Our computer programs make creating snazzy calendars a snap. Include writers' birthdays, quotations, school happenings, and tips for writers. A monthly calendar page would keep your information up to date.
- Literary Magazine: Our writing center staff created a Dead Poets' Society and published a quarterly literary magazine.
- Bookmarks: In-house printing on card stock paper will produce a great looking bookmark to share throughout the school and community. Include quotations, advice, or writing center hours.
- T-shirts: Your center's logo with any of the following sayings on them (with thanks to the members of the "Writing Center Mailing List digest" wcenter@edsel.tosm.ttu.edu):

The Writing Center @ MVHS

Hallway Pass

Name_____

Date _____

To _____ From _____ Period _____

Teacher: _____

Two Examples of "Telling Details" to Enliven Your Writing:

Figurative Language, i.e., a simile, metaphor, or other image:

> "shawl the color of dead leaves" (image);
> "hair wiry as a terrier's" (simile).

Juxtaposition, i.e., something surprising or out of place:

> "grandma knitting a flag" rather than socks or mittens;
> "grandma wearing pink flip-flops" rather than old-lady shoes.

The Writing Center @ MVHS

Figure 4-1, Hallway Pass (front and back)

Got the Write Stuff?

Write Here, Write Now

It's All WRITE with us.

Good Writing Comes from Re:Writing.

"How's your paper going?" On the back of the t-shirt: "I'm (writing) centered"

Yeah, write.

Go edit yourself. (I debated listing this one for obvious reasons.)

Writing Quotations

The following quotations about writing might fit on your writing center's hall passes, calendars, or t-shirts:

> Outside of a dog, a book is man's best friend. Inside of a dog it's too dark to read.
> —Groucho Marx

> Writers would be warm, loyal, and otherwise terrific people—if only they'd stop writing.
> —Laura Miller from a salon.com review of the movie *Finding Forrester*

> If my doctor told me I had only six minutes to live, I wouldn't brood. I'd type a little faster.
> —Isaac Asimov

> We read to know that we are not alone.
> —from *Shadowlands*, C.S. Lewis

> Books aren't written. They are rewritten.
> —Michael Crichton

> I'm not a very good writer, but I'm an excellent rewriter.
> —James Michener

> I love revision. Where else can spilled milk be turned into ice cream?
> —Katherine Patterson

Creativity is allowing yourself to make mistakes. Art is knowing which ones to keep.

—Scott Adams

In baseball you only get three swings and you're out. In rewriting, you get almost as many swings as you want, and you know, sooner or later, you'll hit the ball.

—Neil Simon

I'm writing a book. I've got the page numbers done.

—Steven Wright

A writer who waits for ideal conditions under which to work will die without putting a word to paper.

—E.B. White

I do not choose the right word. I get rid of the wrong one.

—A.E. Housman

No tears in the writer, no tears in the reader.

—Robert Frost

A writer should know how much change a character has in his pockets.

—James Joyce

How can I know what I think, till I see what I say?

—E.M. Forster

Poetry: the best words in the best order.

—Samuel Taylor Coleridge

"Tell me a story" still comprise four of the most powerful words in English.

—Pat Conroy

I take infinite care in how a sentence sounds to me.

—Pat Conroy

Write what matters. If you don't care about what you're writing, neither will your readers.

—Judy Reeves

I always know the ending; that's where I start.

—Toni Morrison

I wrote myself out of my writing mood.

—Virginia Woolf

And when I began to write, the one thing that I knew was: Every single thing you do, all the way through, has got to lead to a sound, inarguable conclusion. And so I developed that habit; I wrote the last line first, and I do so to this day.

—Marcia Davenport

A book ought to be an ice pick to break up the frozen sea within us.

—Franz Kafka

I carry my ideas about me for a long time, often a very long time, before I commit them to writing.

—Ludwig van Beethoven

My most important piece of advice to all you would-be writers *when you write, try to leave out all the parts readers skip.*

—Elmore Leonard

Frequently schoolchildren ask me, "Where do you get your ideas from?" The answer, which always puzzles them is, "I don't get my ideas, they get me."

—Robertson Davies

When I was little, the most thrilling words in the language were, "Once upon a time."

—Mary Higgins Clark

Writing breeds writing.

—Donald M. Murray

One of the most difficult things is the first paragraph. I have spent many months on a first paragraph, and once I get it, the rest just comes out very easily.

—Gabriel Garcia Marquez

Loving to read made me wish to write.

—Eudora Welty

Every writer I know has trouble writing.

—Joseph Heller

Your message has to be that the writing center can help a student become a more effective writer and thereby a more successful student. We sold our writing center message with our messengers. At the beginning of the school year, after practice sessions in our classroom, junior and senior writing center student-editors visited the first-year advisee groups (homerooms) to speak about our services. A sophomore apprentice accompanied each junior or senior speaker. The apprentice passed writing center material, including a brochure and bookmark, and added a few words here or there. Mostly, this apprenticeship was the sophomore's training for the coming year.

The final piece of marketing your services is creating a warm, welcoming, and helpful experience. Word of mouth about that experience will go a long way in ushering in clients. Training your student-editors includes evaluating your facility's effectiveness.

Record Keeping

At our school, we tried to keep our record keeping system simple. We kept two kinds of logs: One in the writing center and one with each editor. Student-editors kept logs of the clients they served; they kept these logs in their portfolios:

Editor's Log

Editor's Name: *Victoria K.*

Client's Name: *Matthew K.* Project Title: *Like Father, Like Son*

Date: *10/23*

Editor's Coments: *Discussed Paragraphing. Some were too long. Overall this paper captured me!*

Client's Name: *Josie B.*   Project Title: *Life as Dance*

Date: *10/28*

Editor's Coments: *Discussed sentence variety. Interesting essay about a dancer's life. They work hard!*

In the writing center itself, student writers signed our book when they arrived to work with a tutor or use a computer:

Date	Period	Student	Editor	Project	Teacher
10/27	2	Elisa Z.	Mike A.	English	Buotte
10/27	2	Erica V.	Allison	My Town	Nye
10/27	2	Andy B.	Scott	B-ball	Blackman
10/27	3	Fred	Christian	Life 101	Kiesman
10/27	3	Pam	Melissa	Golfing	Michaud

Our Writing Center was primarily a drop-in center. With permission from their classroom teachers, students came when they needed to during study halls, their academic class, before school, or after school. Consequently, students did not sign up in advance for an editing session. This reality was the product of having a lot of staff (almost sixty at our peak) and a small school of 525 students. Those student-editors who freelanced in the cafeteria, computer labs, or on the soccer bus heading to a match often scheduled appointments with students.

At the end of each nine-week quarter, our more mathematical staffers tallied the writing center sign-in book, created quarterly usage graphs (see Figure 4-2), and I wrote a memo to the principal discussing the weekly statistics. We also submitted figures on per-period usage (see Figure 4-3).

Our student-editors placed their editing logs in their portfolios. When I read and responded to their portfolios, I reviewed these logs to get a sense of how much editing work the student had accomplished. Paging through the editor's sheets and reading the comments helped me come to know what skills I might need to work on with our staff. Believe me, I didn't spend a long time analyzing the staff logs; I simply got an impression of what was happening.

Using the Data

The quarterly totals served as discussion points. We recognized trends of usage and tried to make staffing decisions accordingly. After our first year of operation, I figured out that I could receive a master list of study halls from our guidance department or assistant principal. This master list showed study hall numbers per period. As with most schools, the study hall numbers changed at midyear. At the beginning of a new semester, student-editors shared information about quiet periods and wildly busy ones. These conversations and the statistics helped us modify editors' assignments.

The usage graphs helped me keep my administrators informed and thereby continued to validate the writing center. As you have read, I supplied

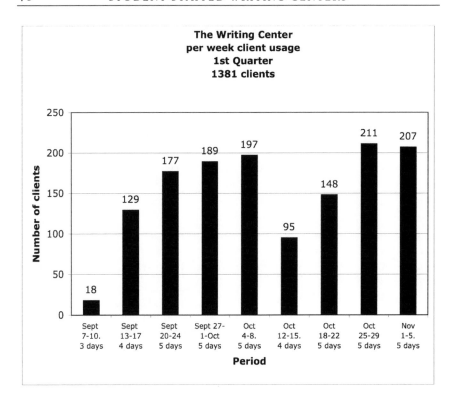

The Writing Center
per week client usage
1st Quarter
1381 clients

TO: Tom Rowe, Principal
FR: Rich Kent, The Writing Center
RE: First Quarter Weekly Usage Figures and Graph
DT: November 8, 1993

During the first quarter of operation, The Writing Center handled 1381 clients. Please notice the weekly totals. The most usage took place in the weeks that had five days of school. The low weeks occurred after Homecoming. As usual, the highest usage came at the end of the quarter— Papers are due! For the 41 days of operation, we averaged 33 students per day. Our 1381 clients were sent from eighteen different teachers or thirty-nine percent of the teaching faculty.

Thanks for your continued support!

Figure 4-2, Quarterly Usage Graphs, 1993

TO: Tom Rowe, Principal
FR: Rich Kent, The Writing Center
RE: First Quarter Period Breakdown
DT: November 16, 1990

The following shows a breakdown of Writing Center usage by periods for our first quarter. As you know, we are not staffed every period (*indicates closed), but some periods an editor found time to be available. Also, please remember we were open for only seven weeks.

1st Quarter Per-Period Breakdown (7 weeks)

Period	Students/Week	Students/Quarter	Per cent
7:30–8a.m.	5.0	35	7.08%
Period 1*	3.5	25	5.06%
Period 2	19.0	133	26.92%
Period 3	6.8	48	9.71%
Period 4*	1.8	13	2.63%
Period 5	8.8	62	12.55%
Period 6	13.7	96	19.43%
Period 7*	2.1	15	3.03%
2:30–3:00pm	9.5	67	13.56%
TOTALS:	**70.2** Students per week	**494** Total number of students	

Compiled by Chris Larsen, MVHS Writing Center Staff

Figure 4-3, Memo to Principal with Per-Period Statistics, 1990

a short analysis of the figures for our principal and the assistant. Because of the mass of paperwork administrators face, I did my best to keep the statistics and figures short and precise.

One caveat: It is a political act to publish the number of students per teacher who use writing center services. I know the politics firsthand because I did this once. Those figures might look something like this:

Teacher	Number of Students	Subject
Mr. MacIsaac	234	English
Ms. Briggs	86	Science
Mr. Kiesman	123	History
Mr. Marvel	3	English
Ms. Consters	72	English

Now imagine that you're Mr. Marvel. Publishing his usage figures could cause some folks to make assumptions about Mr. Marvel's class. They might question the amount of work kids do or the level of rigor. My advice is to keep these usage figures private—writing center directors might use these figures to target certain teachers for conversations about the center's services. Remember, though, we don't know what's happening in a teacher's class until we speak with the teacher: Mr. Marvel's students may be working on revision in writing groups or his students may be partnered with a local college's English class—we just never know.

Other Benefits of Examining the Data

Writing center logs can also provide a glimpse of your school's writing practices. It's a glimpse because only a certain percentage of your faculty and students utilize the services. Publishing figures on the different kinds of writing being done in school might help teachers and administers think more about state-wide test scores, reports from former students about their successes or challenges in college and/or in the workforce, and what kinds of writing might be neglected at school. Writing center directors might publish a document that highlights information such as the data in Figure 4–4.

If a school's leadership team, principal, or department heads were trying to analyze the school's writing program and/or offerings, the figures above will be helpful data, especially when coupled with standardized test scores and teacher anecdotes. The school personnel might ask questions or make observations such as the following:

- Are we providing enough instruction on resume writing?
- Are we providing enough instruction on letter writing? Since compare/contrast writing is a common prompt in standardized tests, should we offer more?
- Are we allowing or encouraging enough of our students to explore creative writing?

	Quarters			
Kinds of Writing	1st Q	2nd Q	3rd Q	4thQ
Argument............	12%	27%	5%	8%
Narrative.............	18%	18%	4%	3%
Autobiography......	45%	5%	1%	0
Summary............	10%	20%	3%	2%
Paraphrase...........	0%	1%	2%	8%
Literature Review..	0%	9%	10%	7%
Compare/Contrast...	6%	12%	3%	3%
CW*/short story....	1%	0%	3%	15%
CW/play	0%	0%	0%	5%
CW/poem	0%	3%	2%	2%
Research Writing..	4%	4%	30%	38%
Analysis.............	4%	1%	5%	8%
Letter (personal)...	0%	0%	3%	0%
Letter (business)...	0%	0%	16%	1%
Resume.............	0%	0%	13%	0%

* CW = Creative Writing

Figure 4-4, Kinds of Writing seen in The Writing Center

- Autobiography is a critical form of written expression; it seems neglected after the first quarter of the year.
- Writing summaries is a vital skill; are we assigning enough as a school?
- Writing analyses is a vital skill; are we assigning enough as a school?

Other statistics might offer a boarder lens of your school's writing program or offerings. For example, what is the gender breakdown of writing center usage? During one first quarter we worked with 1,371 clients in our writing center. The gender breakdown was 707 females and 625 males. What did we make of this data? Frankly, at the time, not much. Now, I'd probably interview students who didn't use the writing center services and look for trends, asking questions in response to the data collected: Are boys less likely to seek help with their writing? Are girls more comfortable with the social setting of writing center conversations? The writing center staff was pretty much split evenly (forty-five percent female, fifty-five percent male). This fact raises questions such as: Are males more likely to seek out females for writing center tutorials?

Talking about these and other questions with writing center staff will raise awareness of the many issues surrounding writing center work.

Assessing Writing Center Services with Student-Editor Self-Evaluations

Have student-editors self-evaluate their work in the writing center. These self-evaluations will help tell the story of your writing center. Gayla S. Keesee and Carole D. Overton of the Paine College Tutorial and Enrichment Center in Augusta, Georgia, have developed an online survey instrument that assists student-editors in self-evaluating their work (see Figure 4-5). Gayla explained that they created the self-evaluations in an online survey program called SurveyMonkey.com. "The site allows us to create a variety of types of questions and then will compile the results," she said. "For a nominal fee it will export to Excel, tabulate specific items, etc. We opted for the free version—ten questions and 100 respondents." Tutors in Paine College's center complete the self-evaluation at the end of each semester. The results are then discussed with the center's director.

Tutor Self-Evaluation: Tutor Characteristics

1. Please rank yourself on the following qualities.

(1) Always (2) Often (3) Sometimes (4) Rarely (5) Never

Display a positive attitude..............................1   2   3   4   5

Provide creative suggestions 1   2   3   4   5

Comfortable with the subject 1   2   3   4   5

Demonstrate knowledge of resources,
techniques, tips...1   2   3   4   5

Adapt easily to different tutoring
situations...1   2   3   4   5

Exhibit patience and understanding.............1   2   3   4   5

Am prepared for each tutoring session.........1   2   3   4   5

Try to follow the steps of the tutoring 1   2   3   4   5

Cycle during each tutoring session 1   2   3   4   5

Encourage students to take responsibility
for their own learning 1   2   3   4   5

Purposefully direct the tutoring session:
ask questions, verify perceptions, praise,
paraphrase, move the session, keep the
student on task, and allow the student to
learn at his/her own pace 1   2   3   4   5

Strive to build the student's self-esteem
and confidence...1   2   3   4   5

Exhibit awareness of and appreciation
for diversity...1   2   3   4   5

Tutor Self-Evaluation: The Tutoring Experience

Please evaluate your effectiveness as a tutor.

(1) Excellent (2) Good (3) Okay (4) Below Average (5) Poor

I ask appropriate questions.............................1   2   3   4   5

I listen to my writers and
provide appropriate feedback.........................1   2   3   4   5

I use writing center resources
(i.e., textbooks, videos, books,
handouts) to effectively assist students............1   2   3   4   5

I understand and employ a
variety of tutoring/teaching strategies.............1   2   3   4   5

I encourage my students to
use good study skills/practices........................1   2   3   4   5

I use appropriate problem-solving processes..........1   2   3   4 5

I use knowledge of effective verbal
and nonverbal communication techniques
to foster active inquiry, collaboration, and
supportive interaction in the tutoring session.......1   2   3   4 5

I adapt teaching methods to the
different learning styles of my students...................1 2   3   4 5

I continually evaluate the effects
of my interaction on my students...........................1 2   3   4 5

I actively seek out
opportunities to become a better tutor..................1 2   3   4 5

Please evaluate how well you follow your assigned work schedule and complete requirements/assignments.

(1) Excellent (2) Good (3) Okay (4) Below Average (5) Poor

I work my scheduled hours..1 2 3   4   5

I am punctual..1 2 3   4   5

I inform my supervisor when
I will be late..1 2 3   4   5

I inform my supervisor when
I cannot come to work..1 2 3   4   5

I turn in my tutoring forms on time.........................1 2 3   4   5

I complete tutor training assignments
(discussion board, Master Tutor project,
video tapes, etc.) in a timely fashion
as required...1 2 3   4   5

I complete all required forms on time.................... 1 2 3   4   5

I keep my Tutoring Attendance and Tutoring
Session Summary Sheets up to date................................1 2 3 4 5

I always wear my TEC name badge
when I am working in the writing center......................1 2 3 4 5

I wear my TEC shirt every Monday................................1 2 3 4 5

Please evaluate your ability to maintain professional relationships with students, other tutors, staff, and supervisors.

(1) Always (2) Often (3) Sometimes (4) Rarely (5) Never

I maintain objectivity with students.............................1 2 3 4 5

I hold appropriate conversations
with students, tutors, and staff.....................................1 2 3 4 5

I understand and meet the
expectations of the academic environment..................1 2 3 4 5

I go through appropriate channels
to report problems and concerns.................................1 2 3 4 5

I behave in a professional
manner while in the writing center 1 2 3 4 5

I show respect for others
who are using the writing center 1 2 3 4 5

I show respect for my students and treat their
situations with confidentiality......................................1 2 3 4 5

I keep my talking at a low level
so that I do not disturb others
who are working in the writing center 1 2 3 4 5

I conduct myself in a professional
manner when I am representing
the writing center 1 2 3 4 5

Skills and Techniques

What approaches to tutoring worked best for you and your writing students?

Please describe methods you employ to enhance your tutoring skills and improve your tutoring technique:

What do you feel you need to work on as a tutor? What skills or knowledge would you like to work on in the future?

Tutor Training

Please indicate the degree to which you agree with the following statements regarding tutor training. Please explain in the comments section if you disagree or strongly disagree with any statement. What suggestions can you provide to remedy this situation?

(1) Strongly Agree (2) Agree (3) Neutral (4) Disagree (5) Strongly Disagree

I was satisfied with my initial training...........................1   2   3   4   5

It was always easy to know the
standard of work expected..1   2   3   4   5

The tutor training sessions
developed my problem-solving skills..............................1   2   3   4   5

I was motivated to do my best work................................1   2   3   4   5

The training sessions made me
feel valued and appreciated as a tutor............................1   2   3   4   5

The training requirements
caused too heavy a workload...1   2   3   4   5

I usually had a clear idea of where
I was going and what was expected
of me as a TEC tutor...1   2   3   4   5

Tutor training prepared me
for working as a tutor in TEC..1   2   3   4   5

As a result of my training,
I feel confident about tackling
unfamiliar or difficult tutoring situations.....................1 2 3 4 5

I felt that my ideas and
suggestions were considered seriously............................1 2 3 4 5

I was generally given enough time
to understand the things I had to learn..........................1 2 3 4 5

The staff made a real effort to
understand difficulties I might
be having with my work and/or
with my personal situation..1 2 3 4 5

Ms. Overton and Ms. Keesee worked
hard to make their topics interesting.............................1 2 3 4 5

Tutor training helped me to develop
the ability to plan my own tutoring sessions..................1 2 3 4 5

Ms. Overton and Ms. Keesee made it
clear right from the start what they
expected from the tutors. 1 2 3 4 5

Overall, I was satisfied with
the quality of my tutor training sessions.......................1 2 3 4 5

Your feedback is definitely appreciated. Thanks for taking the time to complete this survey.

Please answer each of the following questions about your motivation to be a tutor in the TEC. If you need more space, add this information to the final question below.

What aspects of your job keep you motivated and make you want to continue working here?
Is there anything that detracts from your desire to work here?

Is there anything that has made you regret your decision to work in the TEC?

Are there any "perks" for this job that make working here better than working somewhere else?

How would you rate your overall morale, or attitude, for working as a TEC tutor?

Has anything had an effect (positive or negative) on your motivation for working as a tutor?

Other than a raise in pay, which in not something that we can easily arrange, are there any other incentives that could help us boost or maintain tutor morale?

Do you have any suggestions for what we can do to encourage other students to become tutors?

Comments: Please provide any specific suggestions, compliments, or concerns that you feel need to be addressed and that would help us improve tutoring training, the writing center environment, and the program as a whole.

Gayla S. Keesee and Carole D. Overton. Tutor Self-Evaluation, 2004 (www.surveymonkey.com). © 2004. Reprinted with permission.

Figure 4-5, Tutor Self-Evaluation

Assessing Writing Center Services: Client Evaluations

Give writing center clients an opportunity to share their experiences. It's a good idea to keep such tools as simple as possible (See Figure 4-6 for a two-comment survey). Also, a decision must be made to seek feedback on a per-visit basis or at the end of each quarter or semester. No matter when you seek feedback, it's vital to ensure anonymity. Feedback forms could be deposited in a box in the main office, the school lobby, or the media center. The form may also be online.

The feedback from clients and student-editors themselves can be the genesis of professional development activities for student-editors. Faculty- and student-directors can review the comments and isolate the themes and issues that recur. Building an ongoing curriculum from the information will improve the writing center's offerings.

The feedback can also help directors design brochures or other public relations pieces. For example, if a recurrent comment by student writers is "my

The Writing Center Feedback Form

1. The Writing Center student-editor helped me. (Please circle one.)

Strongly Agree   Agree   Neutral   Disagree   Strongly Disagree

Comments?

_____
_____
_____
_____
_____

2. I would recommend The Writing Center to others. (Please circle one.)

Strongly Agree   Agree   Neutral   Disagree   Strongly Disagree

Comments?

_____
_____
_____
_____

Your Name (optional): _____

Your E-mail Address (optional): _____

Student-editor's Name (optional): _____

Thank you for helping us!

Figure 4-6, Client Feedback Form

writing center tutor made me do all the work," perhaps your writing center materials need to further emphasize that staffers will guide and confer, but they won't write the piece.

Faculty directors and student staffers will benefit from professional development opportunities created from outside the writing center. For example, invite a university writing center director and/or staffers to review the client evaluation data that has been collected and create a menu of potential professional development offerings. Invite school colleagues to look at the data and come up with ideas for professional development.

Appointment and Attendance Systems

There are several programs available for making appointments and keeping track of attendance. These programs, some web-based and others downloadable software, speed up record keeping and report development. Two that have been mentioned frequently on the International Writing Centers Association Discussion Forum are Accutrack and TutorTrac.

AccuTrack (www.accutrack.org) claims to be the leading company in administrative software for academic centers, learning labs, and writing centers. AccuTrack launched at colleges and universities in April of 1998. On AccuTrack's website you can take a quick tour that will help you come to understand its capabilities. The company also offers a sixty-day free trial.

TutorTrac (www.tutortrac.com) is a web-based management system. Tutors, students, and administrators have twenty-four-hour access to their records, allowing them the ability to get reports, demographics, make requests, manage scheduling and manage center resource materials at their own convenience. Student writers can search the database for student-editors who specialize in their area. For example, if an engineering major needed an editor who had knowledge on program reports, the student could search for such a tutor and sign up for the tutor's next free tutoring sessions.

These appointment and attendance systems will greatly reduce your paper load, and as with most technology, they will come down in price over time.

Writing Center Websites

You may find that you don't need a website right off, if ever. It's just one more thing to do. However, if you do intend to create a website, check out the various models already online. My advice is to move slowly and perhaps to begin with a welcoming informational site. I am particularly fond of the opening page of Mercersburg Academy's Writing Center (Figure 4–7) written by the late Craig Crist-Evans, writer and founding director of the writing center at Mercersburg.

If you're developing a multi-paged website, you may wish to have the following pages available:

–Home Page

This page could include a photograph of the writing center staff or of the center itself. As with Mercersburg Academy's opening page, welcome everyone!

Mercersburg Academy Writing Center

Dedicated to working with writers at every level of accomplishment, the Mercersburg Academy Writing Center serves the entire academic community. Its mission is to promote writing to learn, writing across the curriculum, creative writing, and preparing students for writing and learning challenges throughout their college careers and beyond.

The Writing Center is a place, but it is more than that. It's an idea, a frame of reference, a way of thinking. Because writing is central to learning at every level, the Writing Center is dedicated to helping students and faculty alike discover the ways in which language and self-expression inform their growth in every discipline. Writing is a learning tool. It mirrors the learning process. Urging students to experiment with form, to take chances with ideas, to allow language to carry them to new horizons of knowledge, to become articulate thinkers and speakers: These are goals of the Writing Center.

The Writing Center offers:

- A place to talk with other students and faculty about the challenges we all face as writers and speakers of English;
- A place for nonnative speakers to explore what it means to learn and think in English;
- A place to bring questions and concerns about assignments in all courses;
- A place to come for assistance with lab reports and research papers;
- A place to share creative writing—poems, stories, personal essays; and
- A place to reach out to the world with writing through publishing and competitions.

Figure 4-7, Mercersburg Academy's Writing Center Opening Page

—Writing Resources Page

This page could include too much. Be careful. The organization of such a site is critical. Review a college OWL such as Purdue's and select among the many offerings (http://owl.english.purdue.edu). Purdue's and other OWLs allow you to link to their site; read about that permission on their website. Again, be discriminating. Less is more.

—Information Page
University High School's Reading and Writing Center has a helpful informational webpage (see Figure 4–8).

—Q&A Page on Writing Center Services
The Reading Writing Center at University High School in Orlando, Florida, offers readers a Q&A page on writing center usage. The following are a couple of examples:

What will the Reading and Writing Center offer our students?
- Whole class instruction in reading and/or writing for all content area teachers
- Small group instruction for students that need extra help with reading or writing assignments
- A risk-free environment for practicing reading and writing skills
- An extensive classroom library of adolescent literature and othet print resources related to reading and writing processes

Are there any other services?
- Information on publishing student work
- Numerous books about wriring and writers
- Computers with Internet access, word processing, and printing
- Extended lessons in teachers' classrooms or in the RWC

—Research Tools and Online Resources Page
Once again, established OWLs will offer a wide variety of areas to link to your website. Themes such as the following will be useful for your student and faculty clients:

—Contests and Publishing Opportunities Page
We all know places locally and on the Web to have our students' work published. Hyperlink a number of different sites to your webpage so students and staff members with deep interests can explore publishing possibilities. The following websites are examples:

Aha! Poetry
Submit, explore, read, and celebrate writing.
http://www.ahapoetry.com

University High School Reading Writing Center

Writing centers attempt to produce better writers, not better writing, through a student-centered, process-oriented approach, which chiefly means talking to writers about writing.

Purpose

The purpose of the University High School Reading Writing Center is to promote literacy appreciation in all of our students and to encourage literacy staff development in our faculty. We further wish to teach students to become independent thinkers, readers, and writers who realize that attention to literacy skills will result in improvement.

We Want Students To

- o   Overcome writing anxiety
- o   Recognize the connection between reading and writing
- o   Recognize and use "good reader" strategies
- o   Read for enjoyment
- o   Learn and practice specific good reader strategies such as questioning, predicting, connecting, and visualizing.
- o   Enjoy the writing process
- o   Appreciate the usefulness and art of writing
- o   Learn and practice specific writing processes such as brainstorming, idea generation, prewriting, drafting, organizing, and revising.
- o   Find their voices
- o   Learn to craft a piece of writing based on its purpose and audience
- o   Develop methods and ideas for revision
- o   Learn proofreading techniques and standard editing symbols

We Want Teachers To

- •   Practice reading and writing strategies with their students and their content
- •   Learn how to begin, manage, and sustain a classroom library and a silent sustained reading program
- •   Integrate reading and writing strategy instruction across content areas
- •   Develop reflective practices by observing, participating in, and discussing whole-class instruction in the RWC

Our Philosophy

Reading and writing skills are connected. Students become better readers by writing and students become better writers by reading.

Figure 4-8, University High School Reading Writing Center Info Page
© Lee Ann Spillane

Teen Ink
As its website explains, "*Teen Ink* has no staff writers; we depend completely on YOU to send writing, art and photos. There is no charge to submit or be published and anything you submit will be considered for *Teen Ink's* magazine, book series and website. Check out our submission guidelines before you submit, including special instructions for sending art and photographs."
http://teenink.com/Submissions

Young People's Press Online
http://www.ypp.net
Nonfiction articles: 500-1,500 words. These can be hard or soft news stories, opinion pieces (limit to 800 words), or feature stories.
Photography/Artwork: If possible, e-mail jpeg/gif of work; otherwise send it by mail (no larger than 8.5 x 11 inches).
Poetry: Three-poem limit per person.
Comics: Send a couple of sample strips by mail (see address on website).
Graffiti: Take photographs of some of your work. If possible, send us a jpeg of it, otherwise send by mail.

The Writer's Voice
http://writers-voice.com
Poems, columns, narratives, fiction, novels, teen humor, short story, drama:
Students may copy and paste their submission into an e-mail.

The Writer's Voice Forum
http://writers-voice.com/Forum/
In The Forum and Feedback Forum student writers may post responses to issues or post their work and receive feedback from participants.

−Writing Center Staff Page
   A group photograph of all of the student staff is a great way to pitch the writing center's services. University High School includes individual pages (see Figure 4-9) for each consultant.

−Faculty Resource Webpage
   You may want to include a wide variety of items, from connections to online lesson plans to links for current professional books. The goal of such a page is to make it immediately useful for your colleagues (see Figure 4-10).

Ben Williams
is a senior at University High School. He's attended UHS since his freshman year as a member of the GIFT magnet program. He's been swimming since his sophomore year and now acts as captain of the swim team. He also enjoys computers and science. Ben spends his free time working at the car wash.

© Lee Ann Spillane

Figure 4-9, Individual Staff Member's Page

FAQs

How does scheduling work for appointments? Are they walk-ins or scheduled? It's good to be able to provide both walk-in service and appointments. It depends on the number of staff on duty per period.

Can students send their papers to the writing center before their appointment? Writing centers have different philosophies and policies concerning prior submission of papers. There's no harm in having the student-editor read a paper in advance if the staff member has time; however, the editing protocol needs to take place with the writer once he or she comes into the writing center.

Faculty Focus

Teaching and Thinking about ...
> The writing process
> Critical thinking
> Kinds of writing
> Technique and voice
>> Grammar and style
> Peer response

Sample writing assignments for ...

Physical education	Vocational technology
Health	Art
Physics	History
Mathematics	English
Biology	Foreign language
Physical science	Technology
Music	

Places to Publish and Calls for Teacher Manuscripts

> Professional Organizations
> Research Sites
> Grant Writing
> Grants
> College and University Connections
> OWLs
> Writing and The World of Work

Figure 4-10, Writing Center Faculty Resource Webpage

CHAPTER FIVE

Working Drafts:
Writing Centers in Action

In a graduate class one day, my teacher James Britton said, "Good classrooms have all kinds of possibilities." The same holds true for writing centers: Everything and anything is possible. Please don't feel limited by my views or experiences, or by the stories of the writing centers to follow.

At our writing center, we never worked to get community volunteers involved; you may. We didn't nurture and expand our affiliation with the university writing center just thirty-five miles down the road; you might like to be more connected to a university. We created separate classes for writing center student-editors; you may not have that freedom or interest. This is all to say, have fun scheming the possibilities of your writing center and develop it in a way that fits you, your school, and your community.

"One Writing Center's Start-up"
Winthrop High School Writing Center, Winthrop, Maine

Week One

It was a Friday morning the period before lunch. A snowstorm loomed on the horizon, winter break beckoned, and the Writing Center "writing coach" hadn't shown up for duty. Even so, English teacher Dave Boardman, the center's volunteer director, was happy with the first week of operation.

"We've had about eight clients so far this week," explained the third-year English teacher.

Housed in the school's library, the Winthrop High School Writing Center began with twelve student writing coaches, a score of blaze-orange info signs posted throughout the hallways (Figure 5-1), a box of writer's materials (e.g., dictionary, thesaurus, a generic "grammar for dummies" book), and one green sign on a makeshift stand: "Writing Coach—Come Up with a Draft!" Dave questioned aloud, "I wonder if that writing coach sign is too big!"

The Student-Run Writing Center

Every period! Every day!

Look for the official "Writing Coach" sign.

Bring your writing-in-progress, ask questions,

talk about writing,

and get input on your latest work.

"It is perfectly okay to write garbage—as long as you edit brilliantly." C.J. Cherryh

Open:
Study Halls
Library Periods
Late-start Wednesdays
Yes! even after school!

Figure 5-1, Informational Sign in Blaze Orange

The previous spring the school board approved the writing center and a portfolio-based, multi-aged English class to be taught by Dave and a colleague from the special education department. Unfortunately, during the summertime Dave's collaborator and writing center co-director from special education took another teaching job closer to his home. Now, Dave was on his own.

Dave recruited twelve writing coaches from his own English classes. One student staffed the center during each period of the 4/4 block schedule in this school of about 300 students. On the bottom of the writing coach assignment sheet, Dave wrote the following message to his staff:

> It is imperative that you show up for your times or talk with me ahead of time. People are counting on you. Please keep track of your work on a daily basis through the Editor's Log Sheets. Remember, ten hours per quarter are required for students taking this class as an honors option. All coaches must document their time for community service hours.

A number of the student writing coach volunteers were in need of community service credits for graduation. Winthrop High School required students to accumulate sixty hours during their four-year careers, and the principal agreed that these writing center hours counted. In addition, a minimum of ten hours of work during a quarter activated the honors option for the class. So, in essence, the kids were receiving credit.

Of the issues that surfaced during Winthrop's first week of operation, the most disconcerting for Dave had to have been no-show student writing coaches. Perhaps the kids simply forgot to leave their study hall for the media center and their volunteer job; perhaps they were busy with their own homework, though Dave had assured them that they could work on their own studies until a client arrived.

Some of the issues Dave and his students faced were similar to issues we faced at Mountain Valley High School. Such challenges are common during the first week, the first year, and even beyond.

"What Happens When Editors Don't Show Up?"

Starting a writing center is like starting a new business; the first few days or weeks of operation set the standard in the eyes of potential student-clients as well as teachers, administrators, and community members. We've all heard it: You only get one chance to make a good first impression.

Our writing center start-up was no different than Winthrop High School's. A few student-editors forgot about or skipped assignments. When it came to no-shows, I held kids accountable. After all, for most of the student-editors, working in the writing center was part of their class work. At Mountain Valley High School, the student-directors or I tracked down missing editors and asked why they had missed their assignment. Naturally, we gave them the benefit of the doubt with their first absence. However, if their absences became habitual, we discussed a lighter load or a different assignment period. Some of our student-editors were so involved with co-curricular activities or after-school jobs that trying to work in the writing center was just too much of a commitment. I helped those students talk about whether they really had time for such an obligation.

Our staff members only had to touch base with a student-director or me to be excused from duty. When possible, we asked for twenty-four-hour notification. Sometimes these volunteers needed their assigned writing center period to meet with a teacher for make-up work; sometimes they required uninterrupted quiet time to study. In most cases all we needed from student-editors was communication.

I explained to Dave that after a few years of operation at Mountain Valley High School, we got to the point where we always had two or three student-editors on duty. Consequently, if someone was absent, it wasn't a huge deal. Eventually, student-editors were charged with finding a replacement for their editing period if they knew in advance that they were going to be missing. Of course, if they were absent due to illness or a last-minute obligation, the student-directors or I would find a replacement when necessary. In rare cases, like at the end of the school day when several student-editors on Academic Decathlon or various sports teams were absent, we closed the writing center for that particular time period. We announced the closing on the written student notices or, if it occurred later in the morning, an administrator would broadcast the closing over the intercom during late notices.

Client Issues: Welcoming and Frightening Student Writers

By the end of the second week of operation, Winthrop's writing coaches had worked with sixteen writers. To learn more about what brought clients in or what kept them out, Dave interviewed several students. Their answers paralleled those I had heard in our center:

"I don't like to talk to people I don't know," explained one student. As Dave realized, some students can be shy about sharing themselves and their work. Making sure the student-editors are friendly and welcoming is critical. Training your editors to be ultra-sensitive to their client's needs is vital.

"She's real smart, isn't she?" asks another. The average kid in middle school or high school could be put off by the idea that certain editors are gifted writers. In both Winthrop's center and ours, a wide range of students served as editors or writing coaches. Dave wondered whether this kind of question found its roots in his heavily tracked school. Kids who have been in lower tracks can sometimes feel intimidated by higher tracked kids. In addition, I noticed that some of our school's higher tracked kids could be concerned about editors who might not be good enough for them. As with

Dave's school, our school was heavily tracked, too. One result of such a hierarchical system is students who are not as open to others as we might wish.

"I don't want to show my writing until it's done," says another. This idea surfaces when kids or adults don't quite grasp the concept of writing as process. They don't understand that all writers' early drafts reveal a lack of polish. It's curious how we act when we hand over rough drafts. When I hand over a piece of writing in midstream, especially to someone I don't know too well, I write this on the first page:

WORKING DRAFTWORKING DRAFT*** WORKING DRAFT***

I've seen published writers, really fine writers who are colleagues of mine, hand over drafts saying, "Now remember, this is a very rough draft. I haven't gone back over this yet to fix it up." Why is it that we are so anxious? Why do we act like 10th graders squirming up to the teacher's desk? Could it be that red pen? As young student writers many of us had our essays mercilessly ripped apart. Our words—our thoughts—were slashed. In essence, we were told we were not good enough. As writing center directors, we must help our student-editors to become sensitive to their roles as caretakers of not only writing but of writers themselves.

When Dave and I corresponded about the work of editors, he was quick to point out that among higher and lower tracked kids "[t]here is absolutely an image thing going on—on both sides.... Too smart to teach, too smart to meet," he quipped. We both worried about the effect of tracking on a student's sense of self as a writer and as a person.

In our global society of the 21st century, should we raise our children in schools that promote such narrow views of learning? With all we know about learning styles and multiple intelligences, shouldn't we nurture and promote egalitarian schools instead of pigeon holing kids according to narrow views of what makes a competent learner? Perhaps this is why organizations such as the following are against tracking or ability grouping in school:

A Sampling of Organizations Against Tracking/Ability Grouping:

US Department of Education
National Education Association
National Governor's Association
College Board
National Council Teachers of English
National Council of Mathematics
National Science Teachers Association
International Reading Association

Carnegie Commission
National Association of State Boards of Education
Education Commission of the States
Council for Basic Education
National Coalition of Advocates for Students
Committee on Policy for Racial Justice
American Civil Liberties Union
Children's Defense Fund

In small ways, writing centers can begin to chip away at the notion that we learn best by being segregated from those who learn differently from us. I love what Dartmouth College's former President James O. Freeman said during his commencement address in 1991:

> It is persons least like ourselves who often teach us the most about ourselves. They challenge us to examine what we have uncritically assumed to be true and raise our eyes to wider horizons.

In the State of Maine, our education commissioner Susan Gendron has spoken out against tracking and plans to make the issue a discussion point among lawmakers and school personnel. For most teachers, the issue of tracking is embedded in the fabric of our schools—it's how we do business. Changing that mindset will be a daunting challenge. Perhaps writing centers can help.

Winthrop Writing Center: Week Three

During the 2004 National Council Teachers of English annual meeting in Indianapolis, I attended a session on secondary writing centers featuring Pamela B. Childers—formerly Pamela B. Farrell, editor of *The High School Writing Center: Establishing and Maintaining One* (1989)—and Dawn Fels, founder of The Writer's Room at University City High School in St. Louis and presently on staff at Fontbonne University, also in St. Louis. One of the words used a good deal during the workshop by Pam was "subversive": A writing center director has to be a bit subversive to build a center's potential. This is to say that we must do whatever it takes, within reason, to keep our centers moving forward. That's just what Dave did during Winthrop's third week as he reveals in this e-mail:

> Hey—one of my students made a deal—I withdrew his detention, and in return he testified before the full student body at Town Meeting this week on how the Writing Center was a good deal. It worked. Editors are often very busy—I've learned a huge amount!! But the big picture is, kids who traditionally could care less about writing

are suddenly asking if they can leave class to go to "one of those writing coach guys." I gladly walk them down the hall. I just realized, I've been talking with kids about writing all day long. This is great.

Pam and Dawn will smile when they hear of Dave's "subversive maneuvering."

Pitching our free services to students and staff quite often means approaching the various players individually. If you had success explaining the benefits of the center's services before its doors opened, you may not have to be much of a salesperson. If clients are lagging, just drop in to chat with colleagues and simply ask, "Could you require your kids to use the writing center for just one paper each quarter?" For those apprehensive about sharing the writing center experience with their students, your approach may be more of a dance: "Is there any way you could help us? Our student-editors need more opportunities working with writers. Would it be possible for our editors to work with your students on just one paper this semester?" For those teachers who are truly reluctant, you might even suggest just one draft of one paper. Having the face-to-face conversation is what's critical, and preparing your student-editors to be at their best would be a smart thing to do.

Call it subversive, political, or just good business, finding ways to connect more students to your writing center is the right thing for you to do.

Winthrop Writing Center: Week Four

"Someone stole the Writing Coach sign from the library!"

"Who would do that?" I asked.

"Probably one of the coaches!" chuckled Dave.

I called Dave on Thursday of week four. We got a good laugh out of the theft. Clearly, the writing coaches just didn't like that big green conspicuous sign.

During the fourth week, the day-to-day of being a volunteer director started to wear on Dave. "It's a huge amount of work to keep the momentum going," he said. "Now that we're near the end of the quarter, our writing coaches are busy with their own work."

Although it's only about thirty yards to Winthrop High's library from Dave's English classroom, walking down the hallway at the beginning of each and every period to check on things is just one more obligation for this busy English teacher. Even though ninety percent of the student-clients are Dave's own students, a breakthrough came when the metal shop teacher encouraged his students to use the writing center's services.

The writing coaches are now filling out a log. Their notations reveal the work they're doing and the difference they're making during their tutorials.

"I read in the log yesterday," Dave explained, "how a writing coach helped a student create more variety in her paragraphs by revising a lot of subject, verb, complement sentences. Not only that, there's been a huge impact on my struggling writers. I could tell that their pieces had been revised and well thought out. It has to be the conversations with writing coaches that are helping them improve. What's great is that these struggling writers knew their work was better and they took pride in it."

These logs, as a history of the center's work, will help Dave and his writing coaches discuss editing and writing center issues. The figures gathered, as previously noted, will help ensure Dave's administrators that the center is viable. The record keeping notations help develop discussion points, questions, and a training curriculum for editors, as revealed in the following:

- "How do I help someone edited a poem when I don't really like poetry?"
- "Where do I find help with MLA citations?"
- "I had this student who was a know-it-all. She only came to the writing center because the teacher made her. She looked at me like I was a drooling moron. Should we have to "help" kids like this? It's humiliating."
- "I am so bad at punctuating dialogue. I need help. Suggestions?"
- "I had this kid who was from the special education resource room. His work was one big paragraph—I just didn't know where to start our conversation."

Ashley: Winthrop's Coaching Star

Dyed hair and black clothes, a Phish t-shirt and early entry into the Air Force, Ashley, a senior, asked Dave if she could join the staff of the writing center. She didn't need the credit or the service hours; she simply liked the idea of helping out. Ashley is a popular writing coach—a field hockey and basketball player; she works three periods a week during first period.

"Ashley's approachable," says Dave. "I think she's involved partly for the social aspect and partly for the writing." At Winthrop, honors track is the top group. Ashley is in college prep, the middle of the academic road at Winthrop.

When speaking about herself as an editor, she says, "Sometimes I write too much, like for comments, and sometimes people don't like that. If that happens, usually they don't come back to me as a coach."

Over the first month of the center's existence, Ashley worked with students from English classes as well as physics and chemistry. The average session lasts about forty minutes. At that time, Ashley's main frustration was that "some kids don't look over their papers at all." In other words, her schoolmates come in with a first-draft piece and expect her to write magic.

Max: Writing Center Blog Coach

One of Dave's portfolio classes is collaborating with Joel Arquillos' 3rd period social studies class at Galileo Academy of Science and Technology in San Francisco. A collaboration with the Bay Area Writing Project and the Maine Writing Project—sites of the National Writing Project—this school community weblog is an exchange between rural students and urban students. Dave has studied the impact of blogging on his students' writing, and his observations are that kids are inspired to write because of the larger audience and the potential for immediate response. Anonymity probably plays a role in the students' motivation as well.

Dave and I exchanged e-mail about the weblog. The following e-mail from Dave captures Max's job as a writing center weblog coach and the future of this collaboration:

> [Max's] mission was to draw students into the overall conversation, especially those who otherwise might not draw a response. This came as an alternative to his previous role as a writing coach in the Writing Center. His involvement ranged from putting questions out on the blog, like, "What's your favorite band," to posting a link to an online test of "Who's Your Favorite Napoleon Dynamite character?" Max logged over fifty entries and responses over two-plus months. While this worked as an alternative, in the future I would give a blog coach more technological power and instruct the person on how to pull someone's entry to the main "Highlights" section. I didn't do that this year because of the pilot-nature of the program. Both Joel Arquillos in California and myself plan to have blog coaches next year who will highlight independent writers and point them out for a larger audience of the general blog membership. We expect to have the coaches converse through a chat room in the blog so they can plan on their level as well. Max has blog-coached somewhat on his own. In the future, blog coaches will be almost like teacher-assistants, or directors/guides for the weblog conversation.

Coaching Issues

A few months into the Winthrop center's operation, Dave says that the honors-track writing coaches "don't seem as approachable and they're too fixated on grammar." Those students who are in Dave's classes and seek the honors level designation are required to spend ten hours per quarter in the writing center as a coach. This requirement seems to turn off these students—they're either too busy or dislike being "told." In addition, writing center usage figures and conversations Dave has had with students reveal that honors students don't want to work with a writing coach. Part of that, Dave thinks, has to do with kids feeling "above the help."

And how's Dave doing in the midst of this start-up?

"I could use time," he answered. "I can see the benefit of being a little freer."

Winthrop's center is struggling now. Visits are down. As Dave looks to the next year, he knows he'll begin with twelve seasoned writing coaches. Training of these students will emphasize a more welcoming posture with an emphasis on conversation, not correctness. Perhaps Dave will use Gillespie and Lerner's *The Allyn and Bacon Guide to Peer Tutoring* (2004) and have his veteran coaches create their own writing center training manual. Summer will play an important role in this soon-to-be fourth-year teacher's thinking as he imagines the potential of his school's writing center.

"Year Three: Building Capacity"
Souhegan High School Writing Center, Amherst, New Hampshire

> The good news about my work is that I get to make it up; the bad news is that I have to make it up!
>
> —Peggy Silva, Writing Coordinator, Souhegan High School

"Every English teacher in the world would want my job!" says Peggy Silva, Souhegan High School's full-time writing coordinator and writing center director. "Our writing center looks a bit like the coffee house from *Friends*. I have two sofas, three chairs—old, ugly, gold, mauve, green, brown—nothing goes together. Kids love it." The center also has a conference area of ten desks and chairs as well as six networked computers. In addition, Peggy boasts, "I have my own copier!"

One thousand students attend this Amherst, New Hampshire high school, and ninety-three percent of them go on to attend post-secondary institutions. "Expectations are extremely high for all students," says Peggy of her school that has doubled in size over the past few years.

Long-range plans are to establish a writing fellows program with students serving as editors in the center and as assistants in classrooms. However, in its third year the center is still staffed solely by Peggy Silva, an English teacher who for ten years prior to her writing center work taught ninth grade on a heterogeneous, interdisciplinary team. During the school day, Peggy serves students and staff members throughout the high school. "Kids make appointments to see me; teachers ask me to teach units in their classrooms. I help seniors with their college essays, juniors with their research papers, and sophomores with their portfolio requirements." In addition, Peggy teaches a yearlong course in basic skills and a trimester writing workshop.

Although she and her center have school and district administrative support—"We are extraordinarily fortunate to have a thoughtful administration and school board which recognize that if we build it, they will come"—Peggy recognized the importance of building capacity and trust in writing center services. To that end, she assisted the guidance department in developing a packet of sample recommendations, résumés, and college application essays. In addition, she works with senior students on the writing component of their senior projects and with teachers in developing a rubric for the junior-year research paper.

This year, Peggy created a staff writing group with the aim of helping colleagues publish their work. "I also offer workshops for English teachers in memoir and nature writing, research various publishing opportunities for my colleagues, and respond to alumni who would like feedback on their first college writing assignments" (Silva, 2004). One of Peggy's primary responsibilities is helping her school faculty and the entire district use a common assessment instrument, 6+1 Trait Writing©. According to Assessment Home©:

> The 6+1 Trait Writing framework is a powerful way to learn and use a common language to refer to characteristics of writing as well as create a common vision of what "good" writing looks like. Teachers and students can use the 6+1 Trait© model to pinpoint areas of strength and weakness as they continue to focus on improved writing.

Monthly Writing Contests

Peggy's savvy approach to developing capacity has been spiced with promotional ideas. "I knew that from a marketing perspective, the first initiatives had to be very public, so I designed a series of monthly writing contests in celebration of writing." For these monthly contests, Peggy developed broad writing themes that offered students the freedom teenagers long for:

> "From the Refrigerator Door"—a piece of writing that students had written for one of their courses
> "Gatherings"—personal narratives or memoirs of seasonal memories
> "To Rhyme or Not to Rhyme"—the writing center's annual poetry contest
> "Witches and Wizards and Elves, Oh My!"—fantasy and science fiction contest

A panel, or editorial board, of students and staff met to discuss the anonymous submissions. Posted on the center's website was the following call for volunteers:

> The Writing Center is looking for staff and student volunteers to serve as members of Editorial Boards that will determine winners of monthly writing contests. Responsibilities include reading and responding to ten contest entries and participating in a discussion of the entries. (Students who have entered a specific contest are ineligible to serve on that month's board.) Students will earn community service hours for their participation. Meetings will be held on Thursdays from 2:30–3:00 in the Writing Center.

During the second year of the Souhegan High School writing center and the first year of the contest, 130 students submitted writing for the various contests. Following each monthly selection, editorial board members wrote letters to the contestants that included specific feedback. During the writing contest's second year, the numbers of entrants fell sharply. Peggy attributes the fall-off to the double-edged sword of being too involved with other writing center work to do the kind of advertising necessary to attract Souhegan's busy students to the contest.

In the third year, the numbers show a tremendous increase over the previous year. The ups and downs of contest participation continue: One contest has ninety entrants thanks to an English teacher who made the contest an assignment; the next month only three entrants. Despite the fluctuation in numbers, the contest has provided an outlet for many students and it continues to promote the writing center.

One other benefit of the writing contests: The students serving on these editorial board panels provide more than writing contest support. Listening to students' discussions, Peggy gets a glimpse into the writing lives of the kids at Souhegan High. For this writing center director who is in the position of guiding the school's effort in writing across the curriculum, gaining a global picture of a school's writing scene helps in the development of planning school-wide writing initiatives.

Website

During this third year at Souhegan High School, the Writing Center's website is little more than a bulletin board of activities and announcements. "I am a novice in technology," admits Peggy. "I carry only a vague awareness of the influence we can have in our small New England setting to affect others with our work" (Silva, 2004). The center's mission statement and statement of purpose are both found on the website (www.sprise.com/shs/writingcenter):

WRITING CENTER MISSION STATEMENT

The Writing Center will foster an active writing community for all members of Souhegan High School.

STATEMENT OF PURPOSE

The Writing Center will:

- Serve all members of the Souhegan community.
- Create opportunities for student writers to work with experts.
- Maintain relationships with state writing resources.
- Encourage and assist students and teachers in submitting work for publication.
- Sponsor celebrations of writing.
- Establish a Writing Fellows Program.
- Encourage online assistance.
- Provide support for classroom teachers.
- Maintain effective relationships within SAU 39.
- Monitor state testing.
- Develop effective writing practices across disciplines.
- Develop a common language for writing assessment.
- Serve as a resource for teachers and students.

As for the future of the website, Peggy says, "Our technology coordinator encourages, cajoles, and nags me to place student and faculty writing on our school's website" (Silva, 2004). But for now, this suggestion is one more item on the center's lengthening "to-do list."

Writing Fellows Program

Souhegan's English Department has an interest in developing a Writing Fellows program based on Brown University's model. The Writing Fellows program will bring trained Souhegan students into the classrooms of assigned teachers. Student fellows will receive deeper instruction in writing and mentoring. According to Peggy, "Fellows would receive an honors designation for their work. We will wait until the Writing Center is operating at full capacity to investigate this option further. Until a majority of teachers request help with student writing, there will not be widespread commitment [on the part of faculty] to working with student fellows" (Silva, 2004).

Q&A

In an e-mail exchange with Peggy, I inquired about several different issues concerning the writing center and her work as director:

RK: What's your writing center's annual client load?

PS: For the 2002-2003 year, I had 350 contacts. About 200 of those were individual students; others were teachers and classroom interactions.

RK: What percent of Souhegan High School students regularly use the center?

PS: I would say that twenty-five to thirty percent of students use the center, but not regularly.

RK: What percent of the faculty regularly require their students to use writing center services?

PS: Alas, an ongoing issue—individuals sometimes require individual students, but the writing center is still knocking on doors to gain support.

RK: What kind of block schedule does your school have? I had a meeting with Tom Newkirk [New Hampshire Literacy Institutes] yesterday and he says your school is known to be quite innovative.

PS: Lots of different answers to that question. School-wide, we have a modified block schedule. Every teacher sees kids for one double block each week. However, teams (grades 9 and 10) are free to plan their own schedules, so when I was on a 9th grade team, I saw my students three times each week for two-hour classes. We have seven teams, so the school actually has eight schedules—very complicated. We don't have any bells, however.

RK: How many English teachers (or other teachers) are former university writing center tutors? Have you tapped them?

PS: None. I have the entire Brown U. curriculum, however, for their writing fellows.

RK: OK, Peggy, tell me a bit more about your job at Souhegan High School. You know, it really sounds as if your position is special. Is your work in the writing center the ideal? How could it be improved? Where do you see your position in five years?

PS: Every English teacher in the world would want my job. In five years, I will know that I have been successful if the entire school uses a common language for writing instruction and writing assessment. We will offer a variety of writing courses to address student needs. Our students, though, do not have the opportunity for many electives. They are very programmed in their studies. That is an observation, not a criticism. We are constantly exploring different ways of using space and time.

The future of the writing center at Souhegan High School shines with possibilities. Peggy Silva's indefatigable spirit coupled with her keen understanding of alliance building—and a supportive administration—creates unique promise for this writers' haven.

Write in the Corner: "Not a Location, but an Experience"
Kettle Moraine High School, Wales, Wisconsin

> When I bring my papers [here], the consultants talk to me about the writing at my level. I understand what to do to improve my writing.
> —Josh, student writer

As Milwaukee sprawls west into Lake County, Kettle Moraine High School swells. Once a rural high school, KMHS is now a suburban school of 1,500 students from ten different communities, creating a school district that spans ninety square miles. The district's focus on writing across the curriculum brought about an 11th grade writing assessment tied to the high school's graduation requirements. A student must score a three on a six-point rubric to be considered a "competent writer" and thus meet the eligibility requirement in writing for graduation.

In the late 1990s, with one teacher and a few student helpers, the KMHS writing center began, in part, to support students through the 11th grade assessment. Now, English teachers Judy Hogan and Joanne Sobolik work as co-directors of Write in the Corner and manage a staff of fifty peer consultants. The co-directors work halftime in the center and half time as English teachers. In addition, two other English teachers have their duty assignments connected to writing center work: one spends her lunchtime in the center and the other staffs the center with peer consultants before and after school. Write in the

Corner is open from 7 a.m. to 3 p.m., offering both appointments and walk-ins.

Judy and Joanne spend time pitching the writing center services as Judy explains: "We make visits to the English classes each semester to review what the writing center can do for them. We meet with teachers from other content areas to explain what we do.... [We] encourage teachers to have us into their classrooms."

In addition, the co-directors present to the school board report usage figures to the high school administration quarterly, advertise the center throughout the school with a brochure (see Figure 5-2), and throw a party for the peer consultants each semester.

"The students like coming here and helping others," said Judy Hogan. "[Being a peer consultant] is seen as a nice position to have. We do provide food [for consultants], which is a major incentive!"

Students apply to become *Write in the Corner* peer consultants. A two-page application form (see Figure 5-3) requires students to self-evaluate their potential as consultants, to write in response to certain prompts, to provide a writing sample, and to supply the names of two teacher references. The co-directors review the applications and speak with the teacher references. Once selected, students receive a welcome letter and are asked to attend a training session (see Figure 5-4).

During training, consultants learn about their responsibilities. In so doing, they also learn about the standards they must set for and demand from their writer clients. Adapted from a workshop presented by Neal Lerner, a chart of responsibilities is included in the training handbook given to KMHS peer consultants (see Figure 5-5).

> Food and fun are the benefits of working in [*Write in the Corner*], but there's much more to it. I was surprised how much I learned by teaching, and it helped me in my own writing, too—especially college applications!
>
> —Erin, peer consultant

KMHS has a traditional school schedule of fifty-minute class periods. Throughout the school day up to ten peer consultants and one faculty member staff the center each period. The work of Kettle Moraine's peer consultants is guided by a four-point document titled "*Write in the Corner* Operations" from the center's handbook (see Figure 5-6).

In conversation with the client, peer consultants fill out a Session Record (see Figure 5-7). This document helps organize a consultant's thinking and also assists the writer in clarifying her or his needs. The Session Records are placed in a folder in *Write in the Corner* and used for data purposes.

**KETTLE MORAINE
HIGH SCHOOL'S
WRITING CENTER**

*Developing Tomorrow's
Writers Today*

Open 7:00 A.M. to 3:00 P.M.

Before and After School
By appointment only

During School
Both appointments and walk-ins
Welcome

Located in the south end of the library
(262) 968-6200 ex. 292

Co-Directors
Ms. Judith S. Hogan
hogani@kmsd.edu

Ms. Joanne A. Sobolik
soboliki@kmsd.edu

in the Corner
Not a location,

but an

Experience

Kettle Moraine High School
349 Oak Crest Drive
Wales, Wisconsin 53183

Home of the Lasers

*Write in the Corner is helpful because they
makes you read your piece out loud and you
can see for yourself if your work makes
sense.*

—*Hope Reddington, student*

THE CO-DIRECTORS

Ms. Judy S. Hogan, who has a Master's degree in literature, has been teaching at Kettle Moraine High School since 1998. She has experience writing for many foundations and school districts. Ms. Hogan's care and desire to see clients succeed is evident from the beginning through the end of a session.

Ms. Joanne A. Sobolik joined the Kettle Moraine High School faculty in 2001. She taught writing and literature for nine years. While completing a Master's degree in education, Ms. Sobolik focused on evaluating writing. She enjoys helping clients become stronger writers, whether they have one or many sessions at Write in the Corner

Ms. Sobolik and Ms. Hogan

Figure 5–2, Kettle Moraine HS *Write in the Corner* Brochure

MISSION STATEMENT

To enhance a cross-curriculum/whole school approach to writing-as-a-process, writing-to-learn, and writing-for-publication. WRITE IN THE CORNER helps all writers identify, understand, and refine their personal writing processes. Write in the Corner staff offers questions in place of corrections, support instead of criticism, and understanding rather than evaluation.

Ms. Judy Hogan discusses writing with Andrea Farfinger

I felt comfortable in the friendly atmosphere of Write in the Corner.
—*Christine Baird, student*

I read my paper to the peer consultants and they gave me a lot of feedback to improve my writing.
—*Carly Chicantek*

WRITE IN THE CORNER PHILOSOPHY

Write in the Corner has a simple purpose: to help you write. We do not edit or proofread for you, but we will help you do so. We do not write on your papers; instead, we advise, encourage, and motivate you to make your own corrections, providing explanations and assistance as the session progresses. We believe that your writing is yours, and you leave the session knowing that you own your work.

OVERVIEW OF A SESSION

When you enter Write in the Corner, a consultant will greet you and the session begins. We ask you about the writing you have brought along and your purpose for writing, or we will help you brainstorm to discover a new topic and approach for a writing assignment.

We listen attentively as you read your writing to us. We only focus on one or two specific areas, such as brainstorming, organizing, or editing, during the session. We ask questions to clarify your purpose and understand the choices you make in your writing.

Before the session ends, we make sure you feel confident to continue making any changes on your own. As you continue to make use of the services offered at Write in the Corner, you become increasingly confident in your ability to write clearly and purposefully.

I enjoy being a peer consultant because my own writing improves.
—*Erin Wilkins, peer consultant*

PEER CONSULTANTS

Because one of the best ways to learn to write well is to teach writing, Write in the Corner relies on peer consultants: students trained to conduct sessions with clients. These are students who enjoy working with you and feel satisfaction when they see your writing improve.

Peer consultants are a valuable part of Write in the Corner because they provide the perspective and insight into your writing work that only your peers can offer.

Client Lyndsey Hoffman answers questions from peer consultant Tresta Greco about her writing.

Figure 5–2, Kettle Moraine HS *Write in the Corner* Brochure

Kettle Moraine High School Writing Center
Peer Consultant Application Form

Please submit this completed form along with your written response to the directors of *Write in the Corner* or your English teacher. The application deadline is *January 15th*. **Consultant training will be announced.**

Please Print

Name _____ Grade _____

Phone Number _____ E-mail _____

List two teachers we may contact as references—one must be an English teacher:

1.

2.

Rate yourself in the following categories on a scale of 1–6 (6 being superb):

___Attendance   ___Knowledge of writing conventions

___Ability to work with others   ___Reliability

___Writing ability   ___Leadership

Print your schedule for this semester, including course title, teacher, and room number:

In the space below list any activities in which you participate:

Please respond to the following questions:

If you had a student with a question that you could not answer, how would you handle the situation?

What do you feel is your greatest strength as a writer?

What do you hope to gain for yourself from being a peer consultant?

Figure 5–3, Peer Consultant Application Form (front page)

Writing Sample

You may attach a one-to-two page sample of your writing on any topic, or you may use one of the following prompts to write a new composition.

In one or two typed pages (double-spaced, of course) respond to one of the following topics.

1. Choose a writing experience that you might characterize as one of the best you have experienced over the years. Explain what causes you to view that experience as positively as you do.

2. Choose one of the following quotes as the basis for self-reflection on your own work/process as a writer.
   a. "There's nothing to writing. All you have to do is sit down at a typewriter and open a vein."—Red Smith
   b. "If we had to say what writing is, we would define it essentially as an act of courage."—Cynthia Ozick

Figure 5-3, Peer Consultant Application Form (back page)

Write in the Corner

February 1, 2005

Dear (Student's first name),

Congratulations! You are a peer consultant in *Write in the Corner*, Kettle Moraine High School's very own writing center. We are excited to begin this new journey with you.

Being a peer consultant is a unique opportunity. Your people skills will improve along with your writing ability. To begin this process of growth, we ask you to attend a one-hour training sessions for all peer consultants. Training sessions will be held on two separate dates; choose the day that works best with your hectic schedule.

Please complete the bottom portion of this letter and return it to Miss Sobolik and Mrs. Hogan, *Write in the Corner* by Tuesday, February 8, 2005.

With warm regards,

Miss Sobolik and Mrs. Hogan

(Return portion below to Miss Sobolik and Mrs. Hogan in *Write in the Corner*)

I will attend the following training session for Peer Consultants.

_____ During my study hall/commons (period)_____
See Mrs. Hogan or Miss Sobolik to determine the date

_____ Thursday, February 10, 2005
(Choose one)
_____ Tuesday, February 15, 2005

Both after school sessions will be held 2:45 p.m. to 3:45 p.m.

Consultant_____
(Write your name here)

Figure 5-4, Welcome Letter

Responsibilities of Consultants	Responsibilities of Writers
✓ Facilitate task ✓ Be flexible ✓ Set priorities ✓ Be honest, yet diplomatic ✓ Be respectful ✓ Place equal importance on interpersonal skills and English knowledge ✓ Find something positive ✓ Serve as a model for approaching the task ✓ Help writers enter disciplinary conversation ✓ Create an alliance ✓ Be on time ✓ Negotiate responsibilities ✓ Shift ownership of task to the writer ✓ Listen well ✓ Explain writing center mission ✓ Understand the assignment ✓ Help writer articulate goals	✓ Bring assignment, text, etc. ✓ Bring motivation and openness ✓ Be active, ask questions ✓ Complete assignment and retain autonomy ✓ Be respectful ✓ Transfer knowledge across tasks and disciplines ✓ Have realistic goals ✓ Revisit work/follow up ✓ Remain receptive to criticism while engaging in argumentative discourse ✓ Bring specific goals to session ✓ Create an alliance ✓ Be on time ✓ Be open to new discoveries

Figure 5-5, Chart of Responsibilities

Write in the Corner
Handbook Table of Contents

Philosophy

    a. The writer always keeps ownership of the writing

    b. The writer reads his/her own writing

    c. The writer makes all changes in the writing

    d. Consultants guide the session by asking questions or making suggestions

Expectations for peer consultants

    a. Commit to two to five class periods per week or before/after school

    b. Demonstrate commitment and professionalism

    c. Work to make each session a learning experience for the writer (and the consultant)

    d. Clean up after your session

Perks

    a. A wonderful experience for the consultant

    b. Food

    c. Improved writing

    d. Good company

    e. Space to read and study when you are not working with a client

    f. More food

Conducting a Session

    a. Meet and greet the client

        Introduce yourself to people you do not know

        Shake hands

    b. Complete session record

    c. Ask client about assignment's parameters

        Check bulletin board for rubrics

        Ask where client is in the writing process

        Ask what help the client desires

    d. Listen to the client read the writing

    e. Ask questions about the writing for clarification and to guide the client toward better writing

    f. Explain errors in conventions when appropriate

    g. Ask the client for his/her plans for revisions to end session

    h. Place session record in the folder

Figure 5-6, Kettle Moraine HS *Write in the Corner* Handbook

Session Record

Client Name _____ Date _____

Grade 9 10 11 12 staff

Instructor_____ Course _____

First visit (*this paper*)? _____   Return? _____

Where are you in the writing process?

      1. prewriting

      2. 1st draft

      3. revision

      4. 2nd draft

      5. editing

Desired help/service—circle specific goal(s) for this visit

      1. ideas

      2. organization

      3. voice

      4. sentence sense

      5. word choice

      6. editing

      7. other

****

Consultant _____

Session Notes:

Figure 5-7, Session Record—*Write in the Corner*

Usage statistics reveal the success of Kettle Moraine's writing center. The latest usage figures reveal per-semester visits to be between 1,095 and 1,452 student-clients (see Figure 5-8). Judy Hogan and Joanne Sobolik have also kept figures on a quarterly basis organized by per-period usage by disciplines (see Figure 5-9).

> *Write in the Corner* is helpful because they make you read your piece out loud and you can see for yourself if your work makes sense.
>
> —Hope, student writer

Semester	2000–2001	2001–2002	2002–2003	2003–2004	2004–2005
Semester 1	656	702	1,383	1,329	1,452
Semester 2	820	939	1,446	1,095	n/a
Total	1,476	1,641	2,829	2,424	n/a

Figure 5-8, KMHS Writing Center Usage History

First Quarter Periods	Language Arts Students	Other Subjects* Students	Personal Use	Total Students
1.	86	1	8	95
2.	71	6	5	76
3.	45	6	6	57
4.	58	5	5	68
5.	43	18	18	79
6.	85	17	14	122
7.	53		16	69
8.	54	1	13	68
9.	70		15	85
10.	23	3		26
TOTAL	588	57	100	745

* Including Social Studies (25), Science (6), Math (22), Art (1), FACE (2), Health (1)

Figure 5-9, Quarterly Breakdown 2002–2003, KMHS Writing Center

Write in the Corner and the Kettle Moraine School District Writing Program

> To write clearly reflects the ability to think clearly. To think clearly and convey thoughts in writing is increasingly a necessity in academic life, in the work place, and in one's personal life. The success of a research paper, a brief, or a simple "thank-you" note depends on the ability to communicate clearly in writing.
>
> —Kettle Moraine Writing Committee

"We launched the [high school] writing center at the same time we implemented the writing program," explained Linda Melton, a writing specialist for the Kettle Moraine School District.

"It was obvious that if we were going to set a rigorous writing requirement for 8th grade promotion and high school graduation we would need to provide additional support to students with deficiencies in writing." As a result, the school district promoted the writing center and mailed information about the center's services to the parents/caregivers of high school students. The information was of course important for students who fell below the school district writing standards. "However," explained Ms. Melton, "it was always our goal that the writing center would address the needs of all students."

Kettle Moraine School District Writing Program has designed an integrated K-12 writing program. See their website at the following URL: http://district.kmsd.edu/~writing/writemain.htm. Teachers and students throughout the school district are guided by the writing program's writing process philosophy:

> The writing process is not a straight progression from Drafting to Published Work. As students become proficient writers, they may plan, draft, and then shift back to planning again as they prepare to revise their work. Writers do not necessarily follow all the steps for every piece of writing. For instance, students aren't expected to revise notes, journal entries, or reflections on learning. Similarly, students' understanding and application of the Six Traits changes as they progress. Most children begin writing in the personal narrative or personal expository modes. These are the stories about family trips, pets, and soccer games. As writing skills become more sophisticated, children may combine several modes in one piece of writing.

In support of this philosophy, the writing program committee has adopted a rubric similar to the 6+1 Traits©. The language of writing is used in the day-to-day learning lives of Kettle Moraine students, K-12. That language is also embedded in the analytic scoring rubric and ultimately becomes the language used by consultants in *Write in the Corner*. Such a district-wide program helps create not only a common language but also higher standards.

According to Ms. Melton, "[O]ne of the original goals of the writing center was that it would serve as a resource for teachers as well as students." Consequently, the Kettle Moraine writing committee looked for ideas from the University of Wisconsin at Madison's Writing Center and its Writing Across the Curriculum Center (http://mendota.english.wisc.edu/~WAC). Ms. Melton explained, "The staff at the [university's Writing Across the Curriculum Center] helps professors design good writing assignments.... I believe this is a natural extension of the Kettle Moraine writing center."

Kettle Moraine's writing committee members and K-12 teachers have engaged in discussions across the grade levels and disciplines about what they value in student writing. Ultimately, says Ms. Melton, "[We have] come to a realization that we want to place a higher value on independent thought in student writing. Some teachers have responded with innovative assignments, particularly in math, but others have not." The district has committed to continued staff development and to developing ways to assess student learning.

The Kettle Moraine district writing program requires students from kindergarten through 12th grade to create writing samples for their work portfolios. Students include a minimum of thirteen writing samples per year. At the end of the year, teachers assist students in identifying four samples to be included in district "passport folios." For students from kindergarten through middle school who struggle, support is available both during the school year and in the summer through special writing courses. High school students may also attend summer writing courses, and during the school year they may also visit the writing center.

The district writing program also sponsored a writing course for district teachers. The course helped teachers develop their own personal writing as well as effective writing assignments for their students. The course assists teachers in utilizing the district's common rubrics and helps teachers recognize what effective writing is.

As a result of the district's efforts to coordinate K-12 writing, ultimately called *Getting Writing Right*, the Kettle Moraine program received a 2004 Magna Award from *The American School Board Journal*. In addition, says Ms. Melton, Kettle Moraine students are scoring above the state average in all areas of the Wisconsin Knowledge and Concepts Exam.

FAQs

How much funding would a typical writing center need?

It depends.

Let's say you took the route that Dave Boardman did in Winthrop: A table in the media center, student coaches from Dave's classes, a few books for student coaches, and a volunteer director. Or perhaps you'd work toward developing a center such as Peggy Silva's at Souhegan High School. She's a full-time teacher and spends her days supporting student and staff writing needs. The school district has wisely invested in Peggy and her large, quirky room!

When we began our student-staffed writing center, my assistant director and I were given one and two course releases respectively. That changed after the first year. I began volunteering, but I was relieved from various teaching duties (e.g., cafeteria duty, study hall) as writing center director. So again, funding depends on what your particular school and school district value, and on what you as an interested faculty-director wish to design for a writing center.

What standards do writing centers connect with?

As provided in Chapter Two, the National Council of Teachers of English Position Statement on writing centers is a strong declaration of support. In addition, the National Board of Professional Teaching Standards includes Standard VI Instructional Resources—this standard could be identified with a writing center:

> VI. Instructional Resources: Accomplished adolescence and young adulthood/ English language arts teachers create, select, adapt, and use a wide range of instructional resources to support their students' learning and strengthen their own teaching.

The English Coalition Conference sponsored by NCTE highlights several areas that focus on writing centers (called writing labs by the coalition). In their document titled "Assumptions, Aims, and Recommendations of the Secondary Strand, Institutional Support" (The English Coalition Conference, 1989) three points support writing centers:

1. Provide sufficient equipment and supplies, including duplicating facilities, media equipment, word processing and writing labs, and sufficient books.
2. Provide increased paraprofessional help to reduce teachers' clerical duties, thus freeing teachers to make more student and community contact.
3. Provide fully staffed writing labs with a minimum of ten word processors, type-writers, and other writing resources.

Resources and Activities

Don't feel pressured to offer any extras as you begin your writing center. If I had suggested to Dave Boardman during his center's 5th week of operation to build capacity by sponsoring a writing contest, he would have smiled away a caustic remark. In time, however, Dave and his writing center staff may decide to create a wide variety of special activities and programs to serve their school and community. As Peggy Silva taught us, such programming helps create a community of writers while marketing the center. These programs are also a good time for student-editors and participants. They offer the kinds of experiences that help writers grow and reveal the potential of writing as a way to learn and to serve others.

For more complete and varied lists of activities and resources, visit writing center websites—especially community writing center sites—to see what they are up to. Once again, you may also wish to join writing center listservs, receive online writing center newsletters such as the University of Texas at Austin's Undergraduate Writing Center's "Praxis," and subscribe to Purdue University's *Writing Lab Newsletter*. All of these publications will help you learn the language and inner workings of writing centers. Though most of the sources listed focus on post-secondary writing centers, you'll see that many of the activities are adaptable to your grade level.

Most of all think about your school and community needs by speaking with students, colleagues, adult education officials, community college connections, and town personnel. At some point it would be terrific for you, your colleagues, and your staff to picture your writing center five years down the road: What will the day-to-day be like? What services might your center provide? What community outreach services could your staff offer? Will your staff work with the adult education or community college population? Will you develop an annex of your writing center in the public library? The possibilities and promise of writing center services across the community open many avenues for exploration.

Resources

Beyond a place for writers to speak with fellow writers, your writing center can be a valuable resource to your school and community. To utilize your human resources, identify writing center staff members' expertise areas: "Lincoln is our digital storytelling expert"; "Cari knows iMovie inside and out"; "Pete does poetry." Have your star moviemaker or poet offer workshops at the center. Publish their work in the writing center to provide models for students and staff. The following is a list of resources you may wish to create for your center:

Model Papers
Supplying model papers to students helps them come to understand the standards and potential of certain kinds of writing. Keep three-ring binders of model papers categorized by subject and theme. Ask teachers across the disciplines to submit copies of what they consider exemplary pieces of writing that students accomplish in their classrooms. Collecting such material could be an assignment for writing center staff who do not have clients during their assignment hours. You could also solicit examples from colleagues in other schools or from online sources. These writing samples do double duty by helping teachers who review them to think about different kinds of writing they may wish to assign to their students. The faculty-director and student-directors should approve the final selected models provided by the writing center. See Figure 6–1 for a partial list of model writing samples that you may wish to have in your writing center.

Sample Writing Assignments for Teachers
Writing Across the Curriculum (WAC) College websites also supply a wide variety of writing assignments in the "For Faculty" sections. You may also find models in the "Resource" sections of WAC sites. The National Network of Writing Across the Curriculum Programs (Elementary-University) is housed at George Mason University (http://wac.gmu.edu/national/network.html). Check out some of these very useful WAC sites for writing assignments and a variety of other writing center resources:

Northern Illinois University (http://www.engl.niu.edu/wac)
Richmond University (http://writing.richmond.edu/wac)
University of Toledo (http://writingcenter.utoledo.edu/wac.htm)
Georgia State University (http://wac.gsu.edu/index.shtml)
Purdue University (http://owl.english.purdue.edu/handouts/WAC)
Massachusetts Institute of Technology (http://web.mit.edu/wac/about.html)

Advertisements
Affidavits
Annotated
bibliographies
Applications
(college)
Applications (jobs)
Applications
(scholarships)
Arguments
Autobiographies
Autopsies
Biographies
Book reviews
Brochures
Business letters
Captions
Cartoons
Commentaries
Commercials
Compare/Contrast
Condolence letters
Contracts
Credos
Critiques
Database
Diagnoses
Dialog
Digital stories
Directions
Editorials
Encyclopedia
articles
Essays
Eulogies
Evaluations
Feasibility studies

Grants
Graphic novels
Historical fiction
Interviews
Jokes
Journals
Letters
Letters of complaint
Letters of
introduction
Literary analysis
Literature reviews
Magazine feature
articles
Manuals
Marketing analyses
Memoirs
Memos
Minutes
Mission Statements
Multi-genre essays
Multi-genre
hypertext essay
Multi-genre research
papers
News articles
Newsletters
Novellas
Observations
Pamphlets
Philosophy of life
Plays
Poems
Political speech
Portfolios
PowerPoint models
Proposals

Reading logs
Requests
Research papers
Response to
literature
Responses
Resumes
Rules
SAT prompts and
essays
School or district
writing assessment
prompts and essays
Scientific labs
Scientific research
reports
Screenplays
Scripts
Self-evaluations
Songs
Speeches
Sports articles
State writing
assessment prompts
and essays
Stories
Summaries
Surveys
Synthesis
Tables/Charts
Technical reports
Toasts
TV script
Video script
Webpages
White paper

Figure 6–1, Model Writing Samples to Include in Your Writing Center

For different connections and information at the middle/secondary level by a 6th-12th grade writing center director, read Pamela B. Childer's online column focused on WAC and CAC (communication across the curriculum) *WAC, CAC, and Writing Centers in Secondary Education* at "Academic Writing: Interdisciplinary Perspectives on Communication Across the Curriculum" at http://wac.colostate.edu/aw/secondary.

English-Language Learners: Information and Study Guides
TOEFL (Test of English as a Foreign Language) and TSE (Test of Spoken English) materials are available through ETS (Educational Testing Services). You may wish to have study materials available for your English-language learners. Exchange students who are thinking about attending a US university would especially appreciate such a resource. Check out the Educational Testing Service website for TOEFL (http://www.ets.org/toefl) and decide what materials might be appropriate for your students.

Create a Writing Center Library
My own classroom library, including many resource books, swelled to 2,500 books through the following:

- Write to parents/caregivers to ask if they have books that they would like to donate.
- Offer extra credit to students who donate books, new or used.
- Drop by yard and garage sales—boxes of books often cost next to nothing.
- Visit the local library—ten-cent used book sales happen every day.
- Connect with used bookstores in search of bargains.
- Check out the bargain tables at Borders, Barnes and Noble, and others.
- Ask friends, family, and colleagues to donate books.
- Have a student write a letter to the local newspaper soliciting books from the newspaper's readership.
- Have the local paper write an article on reading, highlighting the need for books.
- Write a letter to local businesses asking them to sponsor a resource book for your writing center library. Those books can be purchased for $20 to $50. Create a label for the inside of the book, naming the donor—send a copy of that label to your donor.
- Buy online used books at incredible bargains.

Books on Publishing
For serious writers, those who are deeply interested in having their work published, you may wish to purchase resource books. Having such books available will attract a wide range of writers. Consider including some of the following resource books in your writing center library:

2005 *Writer's Market (Writer's Market)* by Kathryn S. Brogan and Robert Lee Brewer.
2004 *Novel and Short Story Writer's Market (Novel and Short Story Writer's Market)* by Anne Bowling et al.
2004 *Children's Writer's and Illustrator's Market (Children's Writer's and Illustrator's Market)* by Alice Pope.
2004 *Writer's Market Online (Writer's Market Online)* by Kathryn Struckel Brogan and Robert Lee Brewer.

These resource books provide thousands of market listings with contact information and submission guidelines. They also include a full year's access to WritersMarket.com. This website provides access to a searchable, continuously updated database of every listing in the books, plus hundreds more (including greeting cards and gifts, syndicates, newspapers, and online publications). Note that used copies of these resource books, even those a year or two old, will save a great deal of money and still offer writers helpful suggestions and resources for publication.

Books on Writing and the Writing Center Library
Collect books on writing (e.g., how-to write description). The following books are a few of my favorites:
The Writing Life by Annie Dillard (Harper)
Digital Storytelling by Joe Lambert (Digital Diner Press)
Because Writing Matters by the National Writing Project and Carl Nagin (National Writing Project)
Description by Monica Wood (Writer's Digest Books)
The Pocket Muse by Monica Wood (Writer's Digest Books)
On Writing by Stephen King (Pocket)
Wild Mind by Natalie Goldberg (Bantam)
Writing Down the Bones by Natalie Goldberg (Bantam)
Thunder and Lightning: Cracking Open the Writer's Craft by Natalie Goldberg (Bantam)
Bird by Bird: Some Instructions on Writing and Life by Anne Lamott (Anchor)
Crafting a Life in Essay, Story, Poem by Donald Murray (Heinemann, Boynton/Cook)

Publishing Outlets for Student and Staff Work
Class, school, district, and community publishing opportunities are available for all writers. Having these ideas and resources available for teachers to peruse will be helpful as they work to enhance opportunities for their students. Such resources transform your writing center into a writers' center that attracts a wide range of folks. Class websites, blogs, and e-mail exchanges all offer free online ways to publish student work from the classroom.

Student publishing opportunities, especially online publishing outlets, often have short life spans. In addition, *beware*: Some publications are scams to have students pay-to-publish. Assign one or two of your student-editors the task of updating your listing of legitimate publishing opportunities. Train these students in scrutinizing websites and publications for rip offs. Some of the legitimate websites include the following:

Teen Ink
A monthly print magazine, website, and a book series all written by teens for teens. There are over 16,000 pages of student writing on this site. *Teen Ink* is now in its sixteenth year of publishing.
http://teenink.com

Merlyn's Pen
At this writing, *Merlyn's Pen* is seeking further funding for its publication services of teen writing. Check out its website to see if it has obtained the necessary support: http://www.merlynspen.org

The Apprentice Writer
Publishes poems, stories, and personal essays by high school students from a thirteen-state area. It has a circulation of 11,000 and is distributed each September. In its twenty-second year, it is edited and produced, in part, by Susquehanna University writing students.
www.susqu.edu/writers/HighSchoolStudents.htm

Writing Contests
As with publications, please be cautious of those writing contests that charge your students to enter. Each year in our local newspaper, a well-meaning community writer sent in a blurb about a national poetry contest. Every person who submitted writing to this contest "won." Their work was published, and they received information on purchasing their copy of the volume—the book cost $69 plus $8.95 for shipping and handling—printed in tiny font.

Scholastic Art and Writing Awards
During the month of October, program information appears on the Scholastic website concerning the Scholastic Art and Writing Awards (www.scholastic.com/artandwritingawards). On the home page of the Scholastic awards, you will see a Virtual Gallery with all of the winners and their works for the past four years. Reading this work and coming to know the standards is incredibly useful.
www.scholastic.com/artandwritingawards/gallery/index.htm

In addition, each year a book of award-winning writing is published in paperback titled *The Best Teen Writing of (the year)* by the Alliance for Young Artists & Writers, Inc. www.artandwriting.org

Holocaust Remembrance Project
The Holocaust Remembrance Project is a national essay contest for high school students that is designed to encourage and promote the study of the Holocaust. Participation in this project encourages students to think responsibly, be aware of world conditions that undermine human dignity, and make decisions that promote the respect and value inherent in every person. Scholarships and other prizes are awarded to students in first, second, and third place categories. First place winners participate in an all-expense-paid trip to Washington, DC to visit the US Holocaust Memorial Museum and other historic sites. In addition, scholarships of up to $5,000 will be awarded to the first-place winners.
www.holocaust.hklaw.com

Model Syllabi: Middle Schools, Secondary Schools, and Universities
Gather a collection of online and hardcopy middle school through university syllabi, lesson plans, or activities that will help teachers recognize the variety of writing and activities accomplished on a variety of levels.

Sample Letters on File
Many books on the market offer model letters. Maintain a collection in your writing center. Such resources will help students, staff, and community members when composing business letters, application letters, letters of complaint, and even condolence:
Over 300 Successful Business Letters for All Occasions by Alan Bond (Barron's)
Great Letters for Every Occasion by Rosalie Maggio (Prentice Hall Art)
The Encyclopedia of Business Letters, Fax Memos, and E-Mail by Robert W. Bly (Career Press)
1001 Letters for All Occasions: The Best Models for Every Business and Personal Need by Cory Sandler and Janice Keefe (Adams Media Corporation)

Sample Prompts and Writing for College Entrance Essays
For students with a study hall and nothing to do: Offer SAT/ACT study sessions called "Practice Makes Perfect" and supply prompts and sample questions. This service could be pitched to faculty members throughout the school. Begin by having resource texts available such as *The Official SAT Study Guide: For the New SAT* by College Board.

Tips on Writing
On writing center bookmarks or hallway passes, posters or your website, share tips on writing. My friend Monica Wood's website offers a series of "Tips for Writers" (http://monicawood.com/tips.html). In addition, your friendly search engine will lead you to countless tips, so will most books on writing. Sprinkle these tips into the school and community landscape; they'll reinforce the notion of revision, and keep the writing center and writing on people's minds.

Posters
To market your writing center, publish posters on 8.5" x 11" or 8.5" x 14" paper by using your school's photocopier. Include your center's logo or an "info" symbol as in Figures 6-2, 6-3, 6-4, and 6-5.

iMovie or Movie Maker Models
For your school's film students or would-be filmmakers, having a collection of finished movies will help them consider the possibilities of their own project. Beyond the finished product, however, it makes sense that the archive of information includes storyboards, scripts or screenplays, "B" rolls, and other models from the movie-making process. Naturally enough, having the entire process laid out for the student will help them frame their own project.

Digital Storytelling Models
As with iMovies, provide a collection of model digital storytelling projects. Some of those projects may be from the Web, including the following:

> The Scott County Digital Storytelling Center
> The Digital Storytelling Center is a collaborative venture between the Scott County Public Library and Scott County Schools, Georgetown, Kentucky. Digital Storytellers meet weekly, Thursday evenings from 5:30–7:30 p.m. at the public library.
> www.scott.k12.ky.us/technology/digitalstorytelling/cdst.html

> The Center for Digital Storytelling is a nonprofit project development, training, and research organization dedicated to assisting people in using

digital media to tell meaningful stories from their lives. Their focus is on developing large-scale projects for community, educational, and business institutions using the methods and principles built around their Digital

The Writing Center

"Instead of Said"

Added	Emphasized	Persisted
Admitted	Explained	Persuaded
Answered	Gasped	Philosophized
Asked	Giggled	Pledged
Bantered	Goaded	Prompted
Blurted	Hinted	Prophesied
Blustered	Implored	Reasoned
Boasted	Insinuated	Reminded
Challenged	Insisted	Repeated
Complained	Interrupted	Revealed
Conceded	Invited	Scolded
Cried	Laughed	Shouted
Defended	Lied	Soothed
Demanded	Mimicked	Teased
Denied	Muttered	Threatened
Directed	Observed	Whispered

Figure 6-2, Writing Center Posters, "Instead of Said"

The Writing Center

Power Verbs

abated	aligned	attained	**C**
abbreviated	allayed	attended	calculated
abolished	alleviated	audited	calibrated
abridged	allocated	augmented	capitalized
absolved	allotted	authored	captured
absorbed	altered	authorized	cared for
accelerated	amassed	automated	carried
accentuated	amended	averted	carved
accommo-	analyzed	avoided	categorized
dated	answered	awarded	catalogued
accomplished	anticipated		caught
accounted for	appeased	**B**	cautioned
accrued	applied	balanced	cemented
accumulated	appointed	began	certified
achieved	appraised	benchmarked	chaired
acquired	approached	benefited	challenged
acted	appropriated	bid	championed
adapted	approved	billed	changed
adopted	arbitrated	blended	charged
added	aroused	blocked	charted
addressed	arranged	bolstered	checked
adjusted	articulated	boosted	chose
administered	ascertained	bought	chronicled
advanced	aspired	branded	circulated
advertised	assembled	bridged	circumvented
advised	assessed	broadened	cited
advocated	assigned	brought	clarified
affirmed	assimilated	budgeted	classified
aided	assisted	built	cleaned
alerted	assured		cleared

Figure 6-3, Writing Center Posters, Power Verbs

The Writing Center
Journal Ideas

o   Name twenty things you'd like to do before you die.

o   Sketch your room and write about it.

o   Write about a person you admire.

o   Discuss what you believe are the five top adult jobs.

o   Discuss the best summer jobs for teen-agers.

o   If you were a parent, what would you teach your son or daughter?

o   Why do you think sports were invented?

o   What would America be like without athletics?

o   Write a letter to your little sister, brother, or young friend sharing survival tips for high school.

o   If you're a hunting advocate, take the devil's advocate position and argue against hunting. If you're against hunting, argue for the sport.

o   Write a letter to a teen-ager who's moving to our town and explain the realities of living here.

o   Write a letter to the principal concerning issues needing attention here at school. Deliver the letter.

o   Thomas Armstrong believes every student is a genius. In fact, he lists the twelve qualities of genius. Write about each quality in relation to yourself: curiosity, playfulness, imagination, creativity, wonder, wisdom, inventiveness, vitality, sensitivity, flexibility, humor, and joy.

o   Sketch a home you'd like to own some day. Discuss the particulars.

o   Complete the following:

    o   I couldn't believe it when...

    o   Back in elementary school...

    o   When —— did ——, I thought that I would...

    o   The best moment in school I've ever had...

    o   When I am asked to read a book I...

    o   The thing that makes me most nervous about becoming an adult is...

o   What do you think the most important invention in world has been and why?

o   Describe the ideal friend in your eyes.

o   What's one of the dumbest things you've ever done?

Figure 6-4, Writing Center Posters and Journal Ideas

The Writing Center
Quotations for Journals!

One life; a little gleam of time between two eternities; no second chance for us forever more.

—Carlyle

The law of chaos is the law of ideas, of improvisations and seasons of belief.

—Wallace Stevens

In life, I have but one simple desire: To tear down the sky.

—Alberto Tomba (ski racer)

The difference between the right word and the almost right word is the difference between lightning and the lightening bug.

—Mark Twain

To a worm in horseradish, the whole world is horseradish.

—An old Yiddish saying

In every crowd are certain persons who seem just like the rest, yet they bear amazing messages.

—Antoine de St. Exupery

If a man does not keep pace with his companions perhaps it is because he hears a different drummer. Let him step to the music which he hears, however measured or far away.

—Henry David Thoreau

I learned to make my mind large, as the universe is large, so that there is room for paradoxes.

—Maxine Hong Kingston, *The Woman Warrior*

Early French aviator Mermoz speaks of the brilliance of flight: It's worth the final smash-up.

—Antoine de St. Exupery, *Wind, Sand and Stars*

After Michelangelo died, someone found in his studio a piece of paper on which he had written a note to his apprentice, in the handwriting of his old age: "Draw, Antonio, draw, Antonio, draw and do not waste time."

—Annie Dillard, The Writing Life

In nature there are neither rewards nor punishments—there are consequences.

—Robert Green Ingersoll, *Some Reasons Why*

Figure 6-4, Writing Center Posters and Quotations for Journals

Storytelling Workshop. They also offer workshops for organizations and individuals and provide a clearinghouse of information about resources on storytelling and new media. www.storycenter.org

Plagiarism 101
A short faculty workshop and discussion on the ins and outs of plagiarism would be a helpful way to talk about writing practices and offer current ideas on this phenomenon. Throughout the World Wide Web countless sites feature papers (e.g., research papers, compare/contrast) that students may access for free or for a price. Such sites support, or promote, plagiarism in some teaching practices. A student need only log on to Free Papers (www.freepapers.net) to obtain a wide variety of compositions—all for around $10 a month. Monster Papers (www.monsterpapers.com) serves up gems. To combat this reality, convince faculty to supply model papers to the writing center (and to their own classes). Encourage faculty to combat plagiarism by:

- talking with their students about it;
- examining and discussing their writing assignments with colleagues to make sure that the assignments are reasonable;
- supporting student writers through the process by utilizing the writing center staff;
- asking students to attach all drafts of a paper to the final copy;
- coming to know a student's voice;
- responding with a letter to students about their papers so the kids recognize the faculty member as an involved reader-audience;
- allowing and encouraging their students to rewrite;
- having students write a good deal in the personal/expressive mode (Martin, 1983);
- asking for and reading drafts of papers in progress;
- forming relationships with students and coming to know their writing, interests, and needs.

Catching Digital Cheaters offers a slew of sites to assist teachers. www.edu-cyberpg.com/Teachers/plagiarism.html

Class Assistants
Student-editors are a great resource for classroom teachers. Perhaps a teacher assigns her 150 students an essay, and she wishes them to have immediate feedback. Writing center tutors could write letter responses. In addition, perhaps one or two tutors can be assigned to a teacher's class and serve as class assistants. During writing workshop these tutors assist the teacher by offering feedback and discussing students' writing.

Blog Coach

Winthrop's blog coach helps keep online sites active, alive, and inclusive. This writing center service does not have to be limited to blogs. Students who write for the school's newspaper will value feedback from writing center coaches. The editor of the school district's newsletter, often the curriculum coordinator, might appreciate feedback or even a simple thank-you note. Any authentic writing experience for writing center student-consultants hones their skills as writers and offers a service.

Research Assistants

My writing center students, student teachers or interns, and former students have served as research assistant for me (Kent, 1997, pp. 160-162). From gathering writing center data to assisting with various research projects (e.g., journal articles, books, graduate class work), student research assistants have helped me handle the large amount of work that faced me as a public school English teacher and writing center director.

Activities

Some writing centers offer a slew of activities; others don't. At ours we offered several. Some were in conjunction with the class I ran for writing center student-editors; others, like our SAT seminar, were stand-alone offerings. My best advice is to discuss potential activities with your student-editors, English department colleagues, and administrators. Also, whatever you offer, make sure it's the best you can make it. Your reputation is on the line each time "The Writing Center Presents..."

SAT Seminars

During the fall, our writing center offered free after-school SAT seminars. They happened ten minutes after the final bell sounded and lasted for just fifteen minutes. I conducted these mini-lessons three days a week for four or five weeks. During each session, students received a handout on the topic of the day and got to take home sample questions and their answers so that they could practice "over their Cheerios" the next morning. The purpose of these seminars was to introduce and/or reinforce the language and the format of the SAT.

I began by getting permission from the principal and then the athletic director. Next, I spoke with or wrote to all of the various coaches and club advisors in the school to make sure it was OK that their students attended and missed, perhaps, the first five minutes of practice. I was acutely aware of time issues because I coached soccer in the fall. The mini-lessons were presented in a large lecture hall in the middle of the school—the hall also happened to be near the gym and that helped football players who had to don all of their gear.

For curriculum, I simply used *The Official SAT Study Guide: For the New SAT* by College Board. Because I was not a math wizard, I asked my friend and colleague Dawn Allen, a true math magician, to present the math sections.

The final activity of the seminar included a practice SAT on the Saturday before the official test in October. We began at the same time as the real test, and all conditions were pretty much the same—the practice test was even given in the same space as the official one. We did not do a full exam because so many student-athletes had matches or games on these late October Saturdays. Students left with an answer sheet to self-score; this pre-exam was extraordinarily popular among students and parents/caregivers.

Working with Elementary Schools
"Bridges": A Cross-age Tutoring Project
My writing center staff, most of whom took their English class from me, worked with fourth and fifth graders in a program we called "Bridges." Over the course of three years, our writing center student-editors visited the local elementary school once or twice a week as a group. After three years on a yellow school bus, I decided to have students do this kind of teaching and mentoring on an individual basis as an independent study or as an extra credit opportunity. Students used a study hall to work with younger students, or the student-editors may have used our fourth quarter independent study project to work as assistant teachers (see Kent, 2000). From editing, co-authoring, and producing plays, the teenagers and their "students" learned from one another.

Bridges created a number of stunning moments, not all of which were positive. The teenagers had an opportunity to observe learning from the teacher's point of view while experiencing the role of teacher, mentor, and older friend. As for the elementary school students, they received one-on-one attention from, in most cases, some pretty neat high school kids. The younger students also had the opportunity to ask questions about life in the upper grades. These conversations, I am sure, assuaged many of their fears about moving to the next level.

Some days in Bridges proved absolutely dazzling. On one such day, my students put on short plays and readings for my friend Greg Waite's fifth graders. Eight stations dotted the hallway, the staircase, and the front lawn. Small groups of fifth graders spent eight minutes at each. One student, Jamie, dressed in full American Indian regalia to tell a story he had created; the eleven-year-olds remained captivated. Other students created an original story in the round using pictures as guides; laughter rolled from the far corner of the hallway. A more reserved student, Matt, read a story about a homeless boy; while another sang folk songs and another read *Green Eggs and Ham* with real green eggs at his feet. This hour passed quickly and the chattering on the return trip to the high school revealed its success. Indeed, a lot of learning took place throughout the whole Bridges experience.

Making Meaning of the Bridges Experience

Near the end of my time at the Bread Loaf School of English, my teacher Dixie Goswami introduced an intriguingly simple yet revealing exercise to help us look more closely at our time together. I used this "making meaning" exercise with my student-editors and my regular English students to help them see more clearly. Truly, this activity gives form and order to what can be chaotic thinking.

Making meaning may focus on any particular aspect of one's class. Among other issues, I have had the students write about working in the writing center, portfolios, and themselves. In the following case we focused on their teaching time in "Bridges."

Here's Tanya's "making meaning" about Bridges. I give my students about a minute for each of the first three steps. The last one usually takes five to eight minutes.

Step one: Using single words name some of what Bridges is to you:
boring
complicated
new
different
challenging
exchanging
sharing
understanding
annoyed
interesting
unrealistic (at times)
regulations
complain
frustrating

Step two: Now name the opposite of those terms to create a dialectic. This is important because reconciling opposites or reasoning contrary arguments helps us arrive at the truth (i.e., there are always two sides to everything):

boring	exciting
complicated	easy
new	old
different	usual
challenging	ordinary

exchanging	quiet
sharing	keeping
understanding	uncooperative
annoyed	pleasant
interesting	boring
unrealistic	realistic
regulations	free
complain	praise
frustrating	easy

Step three: Place some of the opposing words in a true sentence about Bridges:

- I like it when kids **share** their ideas and don't **keep** them to themselves.
- It was a very **fun** experience for me when the children were understanding but at times they could be **uncooperative**.
- Staying at the high school all the time gets **boring**, but going to the elementary school is **exciting**.

Step four: In the final step, we use strict form to help us make meaning. Write one paragraph of five sentences about Bridges using the following guidelines:

Sentence 1 a five-word statement
Sentence 2 a question
Sentence 3 two independent clauses combined by a semi-colon
Sentence 4 a sentence with an introductory phrase
Sentence 5 a two-word statement

Teaching is a challenging experience. Could it be any harder?
I think it depends on our attitudes; all of us need positive attitudes.
Although getting to know these kids was difficult, it eventually
got a little easier. We coped.
                              —Tanya

Teaching was an enlightening experience. Did we learn anything
from this? We teach them things; they teach us things. Once
we got to know them, we became friends. Adventure trek.
                              —Luanne

"Making meaning" helps my student-editors see the full picture. This activity reveals certain truths about issues or ideas. From developing a balanced essay to working out life issues, "making meaning" helps my students think more completely.

Sponsoring Writing Contests

Peggy Silva's writing center in New Hampshire sponsors monthly contests for the student body. Winners receive gift certificates to bookstores and the like. The following are the themes for one academic year:

> Short-Short Stories: Mark Twain once said that if he had had more time he would have told a shorter story. We are looking for the best story that can be told in 1,000 words or less. Staff members are welcome to participate. Deadline: October 1st Awards announced: October 15th

> Simply Good Writing: All genres accepted. We are looking for good writing–fiction, poetry, and nonfiction. This work may be an excerpt of a longer piece. Staff members are welcome to participate.
> Deadline: November 5th   Awards announced: November 19th

> Creative Essay: What's on your mind? Do you have a rant to share, or a humorous look at an event or an idea? We want your voice to be loud and clear in this writing piece. Staff members welcome to participate.
> Deadline: January 7th   Awards announced January 28th

> History Buffs: We are looking for essays that build our understanding of a time period, conflict, or serious issue from our past or present. We hope for representation from students at all grade levels.
> Deadline: February 11th Awards announced: February 25th

> From the Refrigerator Door: This is a chance to earn recognition for a writing assignment you completed for one of your courses–a literary criticism from AP, some nature writing from seminar, a lab report, a research report–any writing you are proud of. We are interested in reading good writing on any subject. Deadline: March 11th Awards announced: March 25

> Poetry: We will accept two poems from each writer. Optional: include an author's statement discussing the ideas explored in the poem. Staff members are welcome to participate. Deadline: April 15th Awards announced: May 6th

Simply Good Writing: All genres accepted. We are looking for good writing—fiction, poetry, and nonfiction. Staff members are welcome to participate. Deadline: May 20th Awards announced: June 3rd

The Souhegan Writing Center website also supplies submission requirements and selection criteria for writers:

How to submit your writing:
- All entries must be word processed on standard white, 8½ x11" paper.
- All work must be of the highest quality; there should be no spelling or grammatical errors.
- All entries other than poetry must be double-spaced.
- Multiple submissions by a single author will be accepted.
- All work must be titled, but your name should not appear on your work.

How winning entries are selected:

- The Writing Center will select the top ten entries submitted.
- An Editorial Board of staff and students will consider these entries and award recognition to three pieces of writing.
- Students and staff members who have submitted entries will not be eligible to serve on the Editorial Board for the month of their submission.
- All writers will receive feedback on their work.
- Winning entries will be published on the Souhegan website and throughout the school.

Note: Students may always turn original writing in to the Writing Center to receive feedback, regardless of whether they are entering one of the contests.

Reading Poetry and Prose at Assisted Living Facilities
Having student-editors read their works or the works of published authors is wonderful entertainment for folks in assisted living facilities. Program directors at nursing homes or the like will be your first contact. Needless to say, these kinds of events bring great PR to your writing center.

Our Stories
Interviewing residents at a nursing home to gather stories for a collection or for a digital storytelling publication is both welcomed by residents and educational for student-editors. If you're thinking about expanding the

knowledge of your student-editors in the arena of digital storytelling, let me suggest Joe Lambert's book, *Digital Storytelling: Capturing Lives, Creating Community* (2002) (see www.storycenter.org).

Literary Café
Student-editors might manage an online site of submissions from students and community members. If it's at all like our school, submissions will have to be approved prior to posting.

Writing a Column for the Local Newspaper
Student-editors love to have an outlet for their own writing. Connecting with your local daily newspaper may create publication opportunities for your staff members. The column could be about writing, could include student writing, or could be simply be the news of the school.

Working with the Yearbook and/or the School Newspaper Staff
Two highly visible outlets for writing center student-editors include working with the yearbook or newspaper staff. Student-editors might help review prose or suggest student writing to include in the yearbook. Having another set of eyes for the newspaper helps eliminate typos.

Writing Workshops
A writing center might wish to sponsor writing workshops such as the following:

> Work with members of an NGO (nongovernmental organization) to revise their monthly newsletter and its publication process.

> Help a social-service organization with the revising of a publication for newly arrived refugees.

> Offer grant-writing workshops for nonprofits.

A Writing Center Newsletter
Publish a newsletter that includes helpful hints, book suggestions, writing assignment suggestions, and statistics. Feature quotations from happy clients and engaged student-editors. The audience for such a newsletter should include students, staff, and readers from beyond the school.

Publishing a Literary Magazine
Our writing center class produced an in-house literary magazine each quarter of the school year. Student-editors selected the pieces included in the

magazine, set up the format, created the cover image, helped with photocopying, collating, and binding, and distributed the copies to homerooms on publication morning. Cover stock paper gives the publication a more professional feel and look.

Pitching Writing Center Services
Speak with the whole school, including custodians, cafeteria personnel, administrative assistants, about writing center services available to them, including resume building, letter writing, word processing assistance, etc. If the interest is there, perhaps the faculty writing center director could offer a workshop in journaling, creative writing, or digital storytelling for staff members.

Fundraiser for Writing Causes
Your writing center could sponsor a "write in" or a "draw in" for a charitable cause such as tsunami school children. A "write in" can raise money on a per-word or per-page basis throughout the community. Sell note cards and invite elementary school students to draw on the covers of note cards. Needless to say, parents/caregivers will accompany their children and these folks are a ready purchasing block!

Writing Handbook for Elementary School
Your student-editors could create a writer's handbook for elementary school children. The student-editors could interview teachers and students from the younger grades to identify critical issues. A combination of artwork and computer graphics could create just the handbook for younger writers. The notion of middle school or high school writers serving as role models and writing coaches to elementary school kids has far-reaching implications.

Writing Handbook for New Students and Transfers
As with the elementary school writing handbook, your student-editors could compile a handbook for first-year students—6th graders in most middle schools and 9th graders in most high schools—and new student transfers to help them come to understand the writing requirements of the school. The handbook could include the following:

- a welcome letter
- tips for writers
- a "free hallway pass" to the writing center for a first visit (address this concept with the administration and the faculty prior to handing them out—could be a pass used only to leave study hall)
- model writing assignments in various teachers' classrooms

- fun writing from student-editors, for example a survival guide for 9th graders and new student transfers.

Movie Reviewers Writing Group

Kids love to offer up their opinions on movies, games, and TV shows. Start a writing group of movie reviewers selected from your writing center student-editors. Approach the local newspaper to see if the editor or publisher would be interested in including the student voice. Other publishing opportunities include the school's website, school newspaper, school newsletter, and the district newsletter.

Writing Buddies

Middle school and high school student-editors could pair up with a special needs elementary school student and share work in person and over e-mail. A model of this program on the university level is occurring between the Colfax School District in Colfax, Washington and the writing center at Washington State University in Pullman. The project summary states:

> This project will modify the current Washington State University Online Writing Lab (OWL), a website (http://owl.wsu.edu) through which students receive direct tutoring on writing skills, to serve special education students in the Colfax, Palouse, and Lacrosse School Districts. The OWL provides one-on-one writing tutoring through a web-based interface, focusing first on development of writers' ideas and voice, and second on presentation issues including grammar, punctuation, and spelling. If the project is indeed successful, it will provide a resource that can serve special education students with writing difficulties state-wide.

Naturally, a Writing Buddy project could benefit any young writer in the elementary grades.

Telementoring

When student-editors mentor peers, younger students, or community members via e-mail or another virtual connection, the student-editors are called telementors. The potential of global telementoring is limitless and could serve to offer your staff members an opportunity to work with students both at home and abroad.

Writing Center Hallway Passes

As mentioned earlier, many schools use passes for students to travel the hallways during class period. Used by the main office, guidance office, nurse's office, and media center as well as individual teachers' classrooms, these passes provide a ready source for publishing student work, distributing writing advice, sharing a good quotation, and offering lessons in grammatical technique. Publish a collection of "The Writing Center Hallway Passes" and distribute the passes to all the various offices and teachers.

Poetry Pass Contest
Similar to Peggy Silva's writing contest, perhaps each month your writing center could publish selected poems on a hallway pass. It's a great way to celebrate your poets and their work.

Community Writing Evenings
Your writing center might connect with a local writer and invite the person to offer a workshop on journal, memoir, short story, poetry, or novel writing. Writers may also present skills workshops, including description, using robust verbs, sentence construction, telling details, etc.

Professional Writers' Discussions
Your writing center might sponsor gatherings each semester that feature writers discussing writing. This event could be solely for teachers.

Informational Workshops on Helpful Websites
Tech-savvy teachers bookmark useful websites. Have a "bookmark share" on the school's server. Create a school- or district-wide "portaportal" (see www.portaportal.com).

SCORE (Service Corps of Retired Executives)
Offer your writing center's services to clients of SCORE. Contact your local SCORE office and explain what your center has to offer.
http://www.score.org

Public Library Partnership
Many public libraries are open in the evenings. Writing centers could team up with the local library to offer poetry readings, writing discussions, resume and cover letter assistance, and other activities for patrons.

University/Secondary School Collaborations
Partnering with a college or university writing center creates a continuum for both middle/secondary student-editors and their collegiate counterparts. The possibilities for such connections run the gamut. The school-based student-editors could learn more about college writing by reading and responding to the work of the college writing center personnel. As mentioned earlier, the college student-editors may take on an independent study or internship in the middle school or high school center. This experience would stretch the college student's understanding of the range of writing through the years and would

allow the students in school to have a connection to that next level of education. For those college student-editors enrolled in a secondary English program or writing degree program, serving as a co-director or intern of a middle/secondary school writing center could add to their experiences, serve as a site for research, and strengthen their curriculum vitae. University and middle/secondary schools could co-sponsor write-ins, writing programs or workshops, author visits, etc.

Bookmarks with Quotations and Technical Advice
Much like the poetry passes, your writing center may wish to publish a series of bookmarks with writing tips or motivational quotations.

Writing Careers Night
Invite authors, newspaper writers, public relations directors, marketing people, sports writers, and advertising people to speak about the writer's life.

College Writing Expectations
A faculty workshop featuring a college professor discussing the expectations and needs for college-level writing is an eye-opener for teachers who believe that writing in college doesn't include first-person writing or assignments such as multi-genre research papers. Perhaps you could invite a writing center director from a nearby university to speak to your faculty.

CHAPTER SEVEN

Conclusion

Final Advice: Join the Writing Center Community

When I began my writing center work in 1990, I called on Doug Rawlins of the University of Maine at Farmington Writing Center. His generosity and skill in assisting my high school students made the kids more sensitive to their roles as student-editors and, quite honestly, as people. I've come to know writing center people at conferences, via e-mail, and over the phone while researching this book. Jon Olson, past president of the International Writing Centers Association, answers e-mail immediately and participates fully in the online mail list *WCenter Digest*. Muriel "Mickey" Harris, the grand dame of university writing center work, edits *The Writing Lab Newsletter* and inspires the next generation of writing center professionals with her generous gifts of time and personal attention. And then just across the parking lot, on the fourth floor of Neville Hall in UMaine's Writing Center, Harvey Kail is legendary. So often as I travel our state a teacher stops me to ask, "How's Harvey?"

Doug, Mickey, Jon, Harvey, and so many others live what I have discovered to be the truth about writing center people: They're magnificent at sharing time and insight. They are listeners and caretakers. Whether you establish a writing center or not, do join the writing center community. Order publications such as *WCenter Digest* and *The Writing Center Journal*. The professional conversations within these publications will help your teaching life in profound ways. Subscribe to *The Writing Lab Newsletter* and listen to the advice of those who guide students through their writing and, in real ways, through their lives. Join the community to enrich your own writing and teaching.

Our Work Together

At the center of it all—both in the writing center and in my former English classroom—were my student-colleagues. These days, hardly a week goes by that I don't hear from one of my writing center "kids," now carpenters, businesspeople, mill workers, lawyers, woodsmen, Ph.D. candidates, ski coaches, actors, boat builders, learning center directors, cooks, electricians, singers, professional snowboarders, mortgage bankers, dancers, engineers, librarians, parents, writers, university administrators, academic advisors, doctors, retailers, truck drivers, biologists, groundskeepers, magazine publishers, physical therapists, and teachers—many teachers.

Together, both while working with the writers of our school community and in our writing center classes, we laughed and talked, argued and discussed, schemed and organized, questioned and listened. Together, we grew to understand that writing and its process inspire with moments that are both maddening and magical.

My English teaching practice blossomed because of my students' daring and increasing confidence as writing center staffers. I believe their daring thrived because of their work as "teachers" in the writing center. Unlike most high school students, these young people enjoyed greater responsibility and authority by assisting our community's writers. They became more connected to the institution of school.

It's common for students to feel marginalized by their school experience. Largely, our kids have one role in secondary school: They receive information. In the ordinary American classroom, assignments are for the most part disconnected to the world beyond the schoolhouse doors; learning styles are ignored; and few wider-world experiences such as apprenticeships and internships occur. What is more, our students are rarely in charge of anything of significance during the day-to-day of school life.

In our schools students move when the bells sound or when the adults say so; they memorize and regurgitate; sit still in rows and listen for most of every school day. This solitary role creates an imbalance in our students' school lives; they're bored and unmotivated. And frankly, with what the 21st century has to offer them outside of school, who can blame them?

Writing center student-staffers have a different school experience. They enjoy opportunities to give and receive, to teach and learn. All of our kids deserve the same.

My writing center students' confidence helped me dare to create a wide variety of activities and opportunities. I share a few of these here as a way of showing what surfaces when both students and their teacher live not only the writing life but also the teaching life.

Class Reunions

On the Friday evenings after Thanksgiving, writing center students, past and present, gathered to read poetry and prose at my home. Former students came back to reconnect with friends and to summon a bit of that writing center *feel*. I'm sure they also came because our little mill town isn't exactly a hotbed of activity for twenty-somethings back from college or their jobs away.

During these Thanksgiving gatherings, former students shared their experiences post-high school. For those who went on to college, a number had become writing center consultants; they offered ideas and piled materials on my kitchen table to help current writing center staff and me. I quizzed all of the students about their post-high school writing experiences. I learned about the writing assignments being dispensed at universities and shared that information with my English teaching colleagues. I heard about the role college writing centers played in dormitories, nearby public schools, and learning assistance centers.

Publishing a Chapbook

Each quarter we published a chapbook of student writing. Each student writer received five copies of the publication and the rest were distributed to our school staff and the library/media center.

Editing Parties

I had nothing to do with editing parties. Writing center staff in groups of four to six or more gathered at someone's home to work with each other. Born out of an immense amount of writing due for our writing center portfolio and the social side that writing had become, these editing parties delighted (and stunned) parents. These students ushered their writing to new levels with pizza, soda, and conversation.

Poetry Garden

The Robert Frost Interpretive Trail near Frost's cabin in Ripton, Vermont, inspired staff member Lynn Lizotte to create our Poetry Garden. Lynn cleared a pathway and built a series of podiums in the woods beside our school. The podiums with Plexiglas covers displayed poems by students and others. Just a suggestion for urban teachers: You and your students might laminate poems and place them on telephone poles, bulletin boards, or building walls if podiums are not possible.

Independent Study Projects

My writing center students' enthusiasm also inspired me to create the end-of-the-year, nine-week independent study projects chronicled in my *Beyond Room 109: Developing Independent Study Projects* (2000). As time moved on in our classroom, it became clear to me that my students craved an opportunity to explore a variety of interests in and beyond our English classroom. These interests were connected to language arts—to reading, writing, speaking, listening, and more—in profound ways. The young people worked in funeral homes and retail stores, on mountaintops and city streets. Their inquiry projects had them building boats, writing plays, choreographing dances, studying Sylvia Plath, and busting down the cinderblock walls of school.

And So...

Clearly, my writing center students gave me the courage to explore the possibilities of our secondary English classroom. These young people became my assistants and my colleagues, and they served the school community in ways that I'm still discovering. With a writing center as a support system, our roles as teachers are redefined.

Appendices

APPENDIX A

SLATE* Statement:
The Concept of a Writing Center by Muriel Harris

(*Support for the Learning and Teaching of English)

The Concept of a Writing Center

Writing centers exist in a variety of shapes, sizes, and settings. Typically they are part of a writing program or learning center and serve the entire school, both at the secondary and college levels. Although writing centers may differ in size, specific services, source of staffing, and organizational procedures, they share the following approaches:

Tutorials are offered in a one-to-one setting

Tutors, who may be peers, professionals, graduate students, part-time instructors, or full-time teachers, meet individually with writers in the writing center either briefly (e.g., fifteen to twenty minutes) or for more extended periods of time (typically an hour) to attend to that particular writer's concerns. The writers who attend the center may come in only a few times for specific help or on a regular basis. Some writers seek help on their own; others appear at the recommendation of teachers; and in some cases, writers work in the center as a required part of their coursework.

Tutors are coaches and collaborators, not teachers

Tutors do not evaluate their students in any way because the tutor's role is to help students, not to lecture at them or repeat information available from the teacher or textbook. Instead, tutors collaborate with writers in ways that facilitate the process of writers finding their own answers. To accomplish this, tutors may engage writers in discussions of their topics so that writers can develop their ideas and practice the phrasing and vocabulary of the kinds of discourses they will be writing. Tutors may also offer reader feedback on developing drafts of papers, suggest writing strategies, diagnose writing problems, ask questions, review misunderstood or missing information, listen to writers, and help them gain a perspective on their writing.

Each student's individual needs are the focus of the tutorial

No two tutorials are alike because every writer is different. The starting point of every tutorial is to find out what that particular student needs or wants. To set the agenda for the tutorial, tutors assess the student's present situation, class requirements, past writing history, general composing habits and approaches to learning, attitudes, motivation, and whatever else is needed to determine how the tutor and student should proceed. Students are encouraged to participate actively in setting the agenda for how the tutor and student will spend their time together.

Experimentation and practice are encouraged

Because learning to write involves practice, risk-taking, and revising, writing centers are places where students are encouraged to try out and to experiment. Removed from the evaluative setting of a classroom, writers are free to engage in trial runs of ideas and approaches, to fail and move on to another attempt, and to receive encouragement for their efforts. Names of various facilities, such as writing center, writing lab, writing place, or writing room, are meant to encourage this view of the writing center as an informal, experimental, active place. This trying-out can be either in the form of talk, as writers practice formulating ideas aloud, or in writing.

Writers work on writing from a variety of courses

While writing centers complement writing courses by providing individualized help, writing centers also serve the entire school by working with writers doing business and lab reports, history term papers, job and school applications, resumes, graduate dissertations, word processing, biology papers, writing contests, and any other writing projects with which students are involved. As writers move beyond writing courses and attempt unfamiliar writing tasks, they profit from interaction with tutors. In schools with active writing-across-the-curriculum programs, the writing center is an integral service, providing the primary source of writing assistance for other courses. Writers preparing for writing competency tests also use the writing center as a resource when preparing for these exams and when brushing up on skills after failed attempts at such exams. In addition, some writing centers provide writing assistance to faculty and staff as well, both with their own writing and with structuring writing assignments for classes. Outreach programs for the community may include workshops for local businesses, grammar hotlines, writing contests, training of tutors for other settings, and conferences on writing. Recognizing that their tutors also learn about writing and gain professional experience in tutorial instruction, writing centers also offer credit courses for tutor training and acknowledge their role in the preparation of future teachers.

Writing centers are available for students at all levels of writing proficiency

Writing centers generally do not limit themselves to working with writers at a particular level of writing skills. Developmental students often have special programs available for them in writing centers, including credit courses which focus on individualized tutorial assistance, but the majority of students using most writing centers are enrolled in a variety of writing courses or courses in other fields. In addition, students learning English as a second language use writing centers to work on writing, listening, and speaking skills.

There are a number of underlying assumptions which guide the writing center's tutorial approach to writing. In the writing center, the uniqueness of each writer is acknowledged as well as the writer's individual needs and the benefits the writer can gain from personal attention. Even when classroom teachers meet with their students in conferences, teachers cannot normally provide opportunities for the extended, ongoing collaborative discussion, questioning, and practice which are the tutor's mainstays. When making decisions about how classroom time is spent, teachers must consider the whole class, and they tend to rely on written comments on student papers as a form of responding to students' writing. The function of the tutor, on the other hand, is to provide nonevaluative, immediate oral feedback, to attend only to that student's questions, and to engage with the student in some active planning, drafting, or revising. The tutor's goal in working on a specific paper with a student is to help that student develop general writing skills. Tutors often rely on asking questions that help students find their own answers, thereby keeping the tutorial an interactive situation in which the student is encouraged to do as much or more talking than the tutor. Numerous studies indicate not only that tutorial instruction benefits writers but also that it enhances their motivation and attitudes. Anxieties about writing are reduced by helpful coaching, positive reinforcement, and the friendly listening ear of the tutor.

In the writing center the writer joins a community of writers. At a time when the field of composing is focusing on the socializing nature of writing, there is a growing recognition of the writing center's role in providing writers with first-hand experience in interacting with readers who can help writers learn about the discourse community for which they are writing. In a room full of other writers, writers collaborate with their tutors, who are themselves encouraged during their training to be actively involved with writing as well. Writers are thus assisted in discarding the antiquated view of the lonely writer secluded from the world as she struggles to communicate with an unknown, unseen audience. Writing centers also reinforce the generally accepted emphasis on writing as a process, for in the center writers actually engage in writing processes with tutors as they learn by doing: How to plan, to brain-storm, to ask questions for revision, to rework written text, to add variety to sentence structure, to organize large amounts of material into a research paper, to proofread, and so on. Two cardinal rules for writing centers are that there be easily accessible stacks of scratch paper lying around and that the pen remain in the hand of the writer.

The Status of Writing Centers

Some writing centers have been in existence for twenty, thirty, or more years, yet the large majority of writing centers at the college level were started in reaction to the "literacy crisis" of the mid-1970s and the subsequent "back-to-basics" movement. Initially conceived as a means of providing supplementary instruction for inadequately prepared students, writing centers were too often viewed from the outside as little more than remedial services or "fix it" clinics where students memorized comma rules and mended fragments. With no preparation and few notions of what a writing center might be, new directors stepped in and created centers as the students poured in. The process has been likened to building a violin while playing it. There was no doubt about the usefulness of writing centers, but they struggled to achieve a respectable status both within the school and among colleagues who taught writing. Despite inadequate recognition of their efforts, writing centers continued to sprout and expand so that, at present, there are more than a thousand writing centers in American and Canadian post-secondary schools and hundreds at the high school level. Today, the most vigorous growth is in high schools, either in individual schools or in whole school districts (for example, see Behm, 1988).

Along with the flourishing number of writing centers has come a recognition of their value as a necessary component of writing programs. Only those truly unacquainted with the functions and benefits of tutorial instruction still view writing centers primarily as dispensers of grammatical rules, havens for inept writers, echo chambers of what has been said already in class, or band-aid shops to patch up bad writing; but such reductionist views do exist and must be contended with. (For one answer to such detractors, see North, 1984.) More generally, writing centers have established their academic credentials and are supported by their institutions.

A recognition of their professionalism and an interest in creating a International network helped to establish the International Writing Centers Association, along with regional groups throughout the United States. The International Writing Centers Association, an NCTE assembly, meets twice yearly at the NCTE and CCCC conferences where it sponsors preconvention workshops and special interest sessions, bestows awards and scholarships, and conducts a meeting of the Executive Board, which is constituted primarily of representatives from the regional groups. The two publications of the International Writing Centers Association are *The Writing Center Journal*, published twice yearly with articles on research and theoretical issues, and the *Writing Lab Newsletter*, published in ten monthly issues (September to June) with practical, immediately useful articles, announcements, and reviews of materials. Regional groups, which meet annually at conferences, continue to be formed. A lengthy Position Statement on the Professional Concerns of Writing Center Directors was published in *The Writing Center Journal* 6 (1985), and the NCTE resolution supporting writing centers appeared in the *Writing Lab Newsletter* 12.6 (1988).

Having come of age, writing centers still find themselves growing and changing directions to fit a diversity of interests. Their flexibility in meeting new needs and their willingness to respond to new challenges cause writing centers to reach out and continually try new programs. Writing centers rarely stay the same from year to year. Their services typically include many of the following: tutoring, workshops, resource libraries of books and handouts, word processing, self-instruction in computer-assisted instruction (CAI), and a variety of other media, writing assessment, grammar hotlines, conversation groups for English-as-a-second-language students, writing contests, tutor training practicums, and credit courses. While most writing centers work only with writing skills, some also offer help with reading, study, and/or oral communication skills. Most writing centers exist within English departments, but others are part of larger learning skills centers or academic support services.

Issues and Concerns

As relative newcomers on the scene of writing instruction, and because of the variety of challenges they face, writing centers confront a variety of issues:

Writing center directors frequently find that those outside the center—administrators, teachers, and students—do not have a very clear understanding of the function of tutorial instruction and tend to think of the center as a place limited to remediation. How can the director educate everyone outside the center's walls? At issue here is the need for clarification and explanation of a nontraditional form of education to those steeped only in traditional formats. Reports to administrators, workshops for teachers, publicity, and invitations to students to visit the center all help but do not always solve the problem completely or finally. Each entering class of students needs such introductions, and teaching staff with large turnovers require yearly orientations for newcomers.

A related issue is that of the status of the writing center. When there is a lack of understanding, outsiders tend to view the center as less important, capable of operating with limited funds and/or facilities, and able to cope with minimal assistance. In times of budget cuts, writing centers are more likely to be viewed as expendable because they are unlike traditional credit-bearing courses. Thus, the tenuous nature of some facilities and their reduced levels of support can demoralize the staff and weaken the writing center's ability to do its work. Where there is a clearer understanding of what the writing center contributes, however, support is strong, and writing centers are likely to be given increased responsibilities. This, in turn, has the potential for creating difficulties in that other faculty may view the growth of the writing center as a threat to their own programs.

Writing centers, because of their variations from institution to institution, do not have a single model to follow or a mold by which to shape themselves. As a result, there are no clear cut guidelines for matters such as administrative structure. Should the center be a part of the English department, should it exist as a separate entity elsewhere in the school structure, or should it be a part of a larger learning skills center? Close ties with an English department ensure coordination with the writing program and keep the teachers and students within easy reach. On the other hand, there are those who see the need for combined facilities to work with all the students' needs—that is, a single center where students come for assistance with reading, writing, and study skills, plus tutoring in other subjects. The tendency toward being swallowed up and losing the writing center's identity causes many writing center directors to argue strongly for a separate existence from any learning center.

The status of the writing center director is not always clear. Should that person be a faculty member or one who holds a staff position? The International Writing Centers Association statement strongly advocates that the director have faculty or administrative status. Appropriate preparation, adequate compensation for administrative duties, and clearly articulated standards for evaluation of the director's performance must be worked out so that the director has a frame of reference for the job.

Although the writing center is normally available to writers in the whole school, there is a need to consider where the emphasis will lie. Will many or most of the students using the center be from writing courses? In a writing-across-the-curriculum program, will the center primarily serve students in writing-intensive courses? To what degree is the center responsible for inadequately prepared or remedial students? The specific responsibilities of the writing center should be defined.

To what degree can or should writers and tutors collaborate? In most writing centers, writers are encouraged to come prepared with working drafts or to spend planning time with tutors. However, where specific honor codes exist that stipulate that no student may help another, the function of collaborative learning must be considered to see if and how it impinges upon this stipulation. Most writing centers do not have this problem; instead, they must deal with teachers' hostility to the concept of collaborative learning because they see it as detracting from honest grades. How much of their students' papers are written by the tutors? Clear guidelines and public discussion are needed. Tutors must also consider the ever-present student request to help with proofreading. To what degree is this a learning experience for the student, or how can it become one? Tutors need to define for themselves the degree of intervention that is appropriate in a student's work.

Because tutorial interaction is at the core of writing center instruction, the addition of computers to writing centers can create difficulties in that hardware becomes the dominant force in the center. Moreover, some writing center directors, while acknowledging the usefulness of providing word processing and computer-assisted instruction, find that administrators mistakenly assume that providing funding for hardware solves the personnel problem; hence, they do not provide accompanying funds for a tutorial staff. However, offering word processing facilities does encourage writers to use the writing center and also counters the image of the center as a place for writers in trouble.

Considerations for Starting a Writing Center

When a writing center is about to be started, the planners must decide a variety of matters:

What will be the writing center's goals?

When a writing center is being planned, it should have some sense of the specific needs it is expected to meet. What initially prompted the creation of the writing center? Who is it supposed to serve? What role is it to play? What need is being met by its existence, and who defined that need? These are typical questions that will help to shape the center's structure and services. Once started, the writing center will grow and change as its role becomes clearer and as new challenges become evident; but initially, the writing center needs some guidelines that will help to determine what equipment is necessary, what materials (if any) should be on hand, and what services should be offered. Typical goals may be to provide more individualized, collaborative assistance with writing, to accompany writing-across-the-curriculum programs, to prepare students for competency testing, and/or to supplement instruction in writing courses.

How can the writing center attract students?

The writing center must set its hours and structure its services so that it is available and convenient for students to use. In a high school or college with large numbers of students who commute, when are the most convenient and practical hours to be open? Will students be able to plan ahead and make appointments, or will they need to have a center available on a drop-in basis? Will students profit from occasional workshops on popular topics, or is the need primarily for one-to-one help? Should there be materials for checkout? Do the students need help in learning to use the library for research? Should tutors be stationed at the library at particular times? Are there student groups that would appreciate workshops on resumes and job applications? Publicity is needed to help students learn about the writing center and its services as well as to learn why it is useful to writers and how to use it. Will students primarily come on a volunteer basis, or will they be referred (or required) by teachers to attend?

Where will the writing center be located?

Should it be near the students' classrooms, in the library, or in the dorms? Writing centers located in the basement of an out-the-way building will have an uphill battle to get students to come in, so the location must be chosen carefully.

Who will fund and support the writing center?

Typically, English departments fund writing centers because they are part of a writing program, but some writing centers receive their funding either from student services or through the office of the dean. Some initial funds may come from grants, and some centers supplement their budget with government funds available for tutoring some of their students. Donations from local businesses or alumni are other sources of extra operating funds.

Who will direct the center and what qualifications should that person have?

The director must be someone willing to assume administrative responsibilities, capable of training tutors, and interested in individualized instruction in writing. Many directors start with little or no experience, but a center will be started more effectively by someone with a background in the teaching of writing, a strong preference and rationale for individualized instruction, and some experience in a tutorial center. Writing center directors are called on to handle a variety of tasks that they may have had no prior experience with, but they need to be or become adept at publicity, public relations, accounting, evaluation, administration, training, and often, grant writing. If their centers will include word processing, they need some familiarity with computers, and they may be called on to judge the effectiveness of having other media available in the center, from videotape equipment for tutor training to tape recorders for self-instruction tape cassettes. Writing center directors need to be flexible, willing to plunge in and accept new challenges, and creative in scavenging for furniture and other equipment.

Who will staff the center, and how will they be compensated?

The tutors may be students, grad students, part-time instructors, professionals, or faculty. Student tutors may qualify for work/study funds, be paid on an hourly basis, or receive course credit. Teachers-in-training may also be compensated with credit for practicum hours, and graduate students and faculty tutor as part of their teaching responsibilities. Some schools rely on peer tutors who volunteer their time, though such students are less likely to keep their commitments to tutoring hours when their workloads become particularly heavy. However, volunteer tutors, particularly those drawn from honor societies, recognize the value of such service on their resumes, in addition to the personal rewards of tutoring. Volunteers from the community and retired teachers have been other successful sources of staffing.

How and when will the staff be trained?

Tutor training varies considerably in the amount of time that can be spent on training. In some programs with shoestring budgets, or with students who have little free time, there is often only a day or so before the start of the semester for orientation. Further training goes on at weekly meetings during the semester. In other cases, schools can have students spend several days to a week of intensive training before starting, or there can be a semester training course for credit before tutoring begins. Training typically includes building awareness of how collaborative learning works, what composing skills are, how writing needs can be diagnosed, and what strategies tutors can use. Training also includes reviews of grammar and help with learning to keep records and to communicate with classroom teachers.

Which materials are needed?

The heart of the writing center is the interaction of tutor and writer, and little is needed for this except facilities for the two people to sit together, plenty of scratch paper, and references writers need such as a dictionary, a thesaurus, style manuals, and some grammar handbooks. Additional materials that may be beneficial are self-instruction work, books, rhetorics, texts and references for ESL students, and other books for writers. Because the focus of the writing center is on the individual, the center should also provide materials that appeal to a variety of learning modes, such as computer programs, cassette tapes, books, and videotapes.

How will records be kept?

When students are referred by teachers, records need to be kept of every visit if the teachers find these useful. Records are also needed to indicate how many students use the center, how often they visit, what services they use, and what evaluation is done. Typically, these statistics are compiled in yearly reports sent to department heads and other administrators. In addition to informing administrators of the writing center's work, such reports also help administrators understand more fully what writing centers do and why they are needed.

How will the staff and services be evaluated?

Evaluation can be made by comparing the grades, motivation, and attitudes of students who attend the writing center with those of students who do not attend; or students using the center, and their teachers, can fill out Likert-type scale evaluation sheets at the end of the semester. Some writing centers ask students to fill out evaluation sheets each time they leave the center. Retention statistics can reveal the center's role in helping high-risk students stay in school, faculty evaluations can indicate how the center is assisting the faculty, and tests for attitudes and writing anxiety can measure gains in these areas.

What types of publicity will be used?

The type and extent of the publicity in large measure determine the success of the writing center, thus calling for creative publicity. Writing centers use ads and articles in the school newspaper and/or radio station, signs around the school and in dorms, brochures distributed around campus and in classes, announcements by teachers, table tents in cafeterias, visits to classes, tee-shirts, open houses, tours, testimonials of previous students, souvenirs (e.g., pencils, visors, balloons, or bookmarks with relevant information about the center), and writing contests.

Which items and personnel should be included in the budget?

To ensure that the writing center is an informal, friendly place, the room benefits from plants, a coffee pot, tables where students can sit side-by-side, and dictionaries and other reference books to use while writing. The center needs a receptionist who can greet incoming students, answer phones, keep records, maintain files of materials, and attend to the upkeep of equipment. Having such a clerical person may seem extravagant, but tutorial instruction suffers greatly when tutors must interrupt their work to tend to such matters. A phone is a necessity when students are likely to call for appointments or use the grammar hotline, as well as for faculty who often have questions and requests. In addition to salaries, the budget must include money for duplicating consumables—such as handouts and exercises—for publicity, journal subscriptions, and writing supplies.

Works Cited and Consulted

Behm, Richard. "Establishing Writing Centers Throughout a School District: A Case Study in Defeating Yeahbuts and Ifonlys," *Writing Lab Newsletter* 12.6 (1988): 1-5.

Clark, Beverly Lyon. *Talking about Writing: A Guide for Tutor and Teacher Conferences.* Ann Arbor: University of Michigan Press, 1985.

Clark, Irene L. *Writing in the Center: Teaching in a Writing Center Setting.* Dubuque: Kendall/Hunt, 1985.

Harris, Muriel. *Tutoring Writing: A Sourcebook for Writing Labs.* Glenview, IL: Scott, Foresman, 1982.

Harris, Muriel. *Teaching One-to-One: The Writing Conference.* Urbana, IL: International Council of Teachers of English, 1986.

Hawkins, Thorn and Phyllis Brooks, eds. *Improving Writing Skills. New Directions for College Learning Assistance, No. 3.* San Francisco: Jossey-Bass, 1981.

Meyer, Emily and Louise Z. Smith. *The Practical Tutor.* New York: Oxford University Press, 1987.

North, Stephen. "The Idea of a Writing Center," *College English* 46 (1984): 433-447.

Stewart, Joyce and Mary Croft. *The Writing Laboratory.* Glenview, IL: Scott, Foresman, 1982.

Originally published by The International Council of Teachers of English, September 1988.
© 2005 by the National Council of Teachers of English. Reprinted with permission.

APPENDIX B

Brief Bibliography of Writing Center Resources prepared by the International Writing Centers Association

History

Boquet, Elizabeth H. "Our Little Secret: A History of Writing Centers, Pre- to Post-Open Admissions," *College Composition and Communication* 50.3 (1999): 463-482.

Carino, Peter. "Early Writing Centers: Toward a History," *The Writing Center Journal* 15. 2 (1995): 103–115.

Carino, Peter. "Open Admissions and the Construction of Writing Center History: A Tale of Three Models," *The Writing Center Journal* 17.1 (1996): 30–48.

Harris, Muriel. "What's Up and What's In: Trends and Traditions in Writing Centers," *The Writing Center Journal* 11.1 (1990): 15–25.

Kinkead, Joyce. "The International Writing Centers Association as Mooring: A Personal History of the First Ten Years," *The Writing Center Journal* 16.2 (1996): 131–143.

Yahner, William and William Murdick. "The Evolution of a Writing Center: 1972–1990," *The Writing Center Journal* 11.2 (1991): 13–28.

Administration, Program Development, and Professional Concerns

Bell, Jim. "Promotional Ideas for Writing Centers," *Writing Lab Newsletter* 21.1 (1996): 1–4.

Carroll, Shireen, Bruce Pegg, and Stephen Newmann. "Size Matters: Administering a Writing Center in a Small College Setting," *Writing Lab Newsletter* 24.5 (2000): 1–5.

Cox, Bené Scanlon. "Priorities and Guidelines for the Development of Writing Centers: A Delphi Study." In Olson, 1984, pp. 77–84.

Farrell, Pamela B. *The High School Writing Center: Establishing and Maintaining One.* Urbana, IL: NCTE, 1989.

Healy, Dave. "Writing Center Directors: An Emerging Portrait of the Profession," *Writing Program Administration* 18.3 (Spring 1995): 26–43.

Kinkead, Joyce A. *Writing Centers in Context: Twelve Case Studies.* Urbana, IL: NCTE, 1993.

Olson, Gary A., ed. *Writing Centers: Theory and Administration.* Urbana, IL: NCTE, 1984.

Olson, Gary A. "Establishing and Maintaining a Writing Center in a Two-year College." In Olson, 1984, pp. 87–100.

Riley, Terrance. "The Unpromising Future of Writing Centers," *The Writing Center Journal* 15.1 (1994): 20–34.

Simpson, Jeanne. "Perceptions, Realities, and Possibilities: Central Administration and Writing Centers." In Stay, Murphy, and Hobson, 1995, pp. 48–52.

Simpson, Jeanne. "What Lies Ahead for Writing Centers: Position Statement on Professional Concerns," *The Writing Center Journal* 5.2/6.1 (1985): 35–39. Reprinted in Murphy and Law, 1995, pp. 57–61.

Stay, Byron L., Christina Murphy, and Eric H. Hobson, eds. *Writing Center Perspectives.* Emmitsburg, MD: IWCA Press, 1995.

Wallace, Ray and Jeane Simpson, eds. *The Writing Center: New Directions.* New York: Garland, 1991.

Theory

Behm, Richard. "Ethical Issues in Peer Tutoring: A Defense of Collaborative Learning," *The Writing Center Journal* 10 (1989): 3–12.

Brannon, Lil and C. H. Knoblauch. "A Philosophical Perspective on Writing Centers and the Teaching of Writing." In Olson, 1984, pp. 36–47.

Bruffee, Kenneth A. "Peer Tutoring and the 'Conversation of Mankind.'" In Olson, 1984, pp. 3–15 and Murphy and Law, 1995, pp. 87–98.

Bushman, Donald E. "Past Accomplishments and Current Trends in Writing Center Research: A Bibliographic Essay." In Wallace and Simpson, 1991, pp. 27–38.

Carino, Peter. "Theorizing the Writing Center: An Uneasy Task," *Dialogue: A Journal for Writing Specialists* 2.1 (1995): 23–37.

Ede, Lisa. "Writing as Social Process: A Theoretical Foundation for Writing Centers?" *The Writing Center Journal* 9.2 (1989): 3–14. Reprinted in Murphy and Law, 1995, pp. 99–107.

Gillam, Alice. "Solutions and Trade-offs in the Writing Center," *The Writing Center Journal* 12.1 (1991): 63–79.

Gillam, Alice. "Collaborative Learning Theory and Peer Tutoring Practice." In Mullin and Wallace, 1994, pp. 39–53.

Hobson, Eric. "Writing Center Practice Often Counters Its Theory. So What?" In Mullin and Wallace, 1994, pp. 1–19

Kail, Harvey and John Trimbur. "The Politics of Peer Tutoring," *WPA: Writing Program Administration* 11(1987): 5–12. In Murphy and Law, 1995, pp. 203–210.

Lunsford, Andrea. "Collaboration, Control, and the Idea of a Writing Center," *The Writing Center Journal* 12.1 (1991): 3–10. Reprinted in Murphy and Law, 1995, pp. 109–115 and Murphy and Sherwood, 1995, pp. 36–42.

Mullin, Joan A. and Ray Wallace, eds. *Intersections: Theory-Practice in the Writing Center.* Urbana, IL: NCTE, 1994.

Murphy, Christina and Joe Law. "The Writing Center and Social Constructionist Theory." In Mullin and Wallace, 1994, pp. 25–38.

Murphy, Christina and Joe Law, eds. *Landmark Essays on Writing Centers.* Davis, CA: Hermagoras, 1995.

Murphy, Christina and Joe Law. "Writing Centers in Contact: Responding to Current Educational Theory." In Murphy and Law, 1995, pp. 117–125.

North, Stephen. "The Idea of a Writing Center," *College English* 46 (September) 1984: 436–446. Reprinted in Murphy and Law, 1995, pp. 71–85 and Murphy and Sherwood, 1995, pp. 22–36.

North, Stephen. "Revisiting 'The Idea of a Writing Center.'" *The Writing Center Journal* 15.1 (1994): 7–19.

Trimbur, John. "Peer Tutoring: A Contradiction in Terms?" *The Writing Center Journal* 7.2 (1987): 21–27.

Trimbur, John. "Consensus and Difference in Collaborative Learning," *College English* 51 (1989): 602–616.

Warnock, Tilly and John Warnock. "Liberatory Writing Centers: Restoring Authority to Writers." In Olson, 1984, pp. 16–23.

Practice

Brooks, Jeff. "Minimalist Tutoring: Making the Student Do All the Work," *Writing Lab Newsletter* 15.6 (1991): 1–4. Reprinted in Murphy and Sherwood, 1995, pp. 83–87.

Friedlander, Alexander. "Meeting the Needs of Foreign Students in the Writing Center." In Olson, 1984, pp. 206–215.

Fulwiler, Toby. "Provocative Revision," *The Writing Center Journal* 12.2 (1992): 190–204. Reprinted in Murphy and Sherwood, 1995, pp. 71–82.

Konstant, Shoshona Beth. "Multi-sensory Tutoring for Multi-sensory Learners," *Writing Lab Newsletter* 16.9–10 (1992): 6–8. Reprinted in Murphy and Sherwood, 1995, pp. 108–111.

Neff, Julie. "Learning Disabilities in the Writing Center." In Mullin and Wallace, 1994, pp. 81–95.

Powers, Judith K. "Rethinking Writing Center Conferencing Strategies for the ESL Writer," *The Writing Center Journal* 13.2 (1993): 39–47.

Peer Tutoring Training and Issues

Bannister-Wills, Linda. "Developing a Peer Tutor Program." In Olson, 1984, pp. 132–143.

Capossela, Toni-Lee. *The Harcourt Brace Guide to Peer Tutoring.* New York: Harcourt, Brace, Jovanovich, 1998.

Cobb, Loretta and Elaine Kilgore Elledge. "Undergraduate Staffing in the Writing Center." In Olson, 1984, pp. 123–131.

Gillespie, Paula and Neal Lerner. *The Allyn and Bacon Guide to Peer Tutoring.* Boston: Allyn and Bacon, 2000.

Harris, Muriel. *Teaching Writing: A Sourcebook for Writing Labs.* Glenview, IL: Scott, Foresman, 1982.

Harris, Muriel. *Teaching One-to-One: The Writing Center Conference.* Urbana, IL: NCTE, 1986.

Murphy, Christina and Steve Sherwood. *The St. Martin's Sourcebook for Writing Tutors.* New York: St. Martin's, 1995.

Rafoth, Ben. *A Tutor's Guide: Helping Writers One to One.* New York: Heinemann, 2000.

Reigstad, Thomas J. and Donald McAndrew. *Training Tutors for Writing Center Conferences.* Urbana, IL: NCTE, 1984.

Ryan, Leigh. *The Bedford Guide for Writing Tutors.* Boston: Bedford, 1994.

Smith, Louise and Emily Myer. *The Practical Tutor.* New York: Oxford, 1987.

Online Writing Centers

Hobson, Eric H. *Wiring the Writing Center.* Logan, UT. Utah University Press, 1998.

Inman, James A. and Donna M. Sewell. *Taking Flight with OWLs: Examining Electronic Writing Center Work.* Mahwah, NJ: Lawrence Erlbaum, 2000.

Inman, James A. and Clinton Gardner. *The OWL Construction and Maintenance Guide.* Emmitsburg, MA: IWCA Press, 2001.

"Online Writing Labs: Should We? Will We? Are We?" *Kairos: A Journal of Rhetoric, Technology, and Pedagogy* 1.1 (1996).

APPENDIX C

University of Notre Dame Writing Center Brochure

© Reprinted with Permission

Bibliography

Assessment home. (© 2001). Retrieved Jan. 24, 2005, from http://www.nwrel.org/assessment/

Brooks, Jeff. "Minimalist Tutoring: Making the Student Do All the Work." *Writing Lab Newsletter* 15.6 (February 1991): 1-4.

Brooks, J.G., and Brooks, M.G. (1993). *In search of understanding: The case for constructivist classrooms*. Alexandria, VA: Association for Supervision and Curriculum Development.

Bruce, S., and Rafoth, B. (2004). *ESL Writers: A Guide for Writing Center Tutors*. Portsmouth, NH: Heinemann—Boynton/Cook.

Farrell, Pamela B. (Ed.) (1989). *The High School Writing Center: Establishing and Maintaining One*. Urbana, IL: NCTE.

Gillespie, Paula, and Neal Lerner. (2000). *The Allyn and Bacon Guide to Peer Tutoring*. Boston: Allyn and Bacon.

Hobson, Eric H. (1998). *Wiring the Writing Center*. Logan, Utah: Utah University Press.

Howard, Rebecca Moore. "A Plagiarism Pentimento. *Journal of Teaching Writing* 11 (1993): 233.

Inman, James A., and Donna M. Sewell. (2000). *Taking Flight with OWLs: Examining Electronic Writing Center Work*. Mahwah, New Jersey: Lawrence Erlbaum.

Inman, James A., and Clinton Gardner. (2001). *The OWL Construction and Maintenance Guide*. Emmitsburg, MA: IWCA Press.

Jefferson Middle School Writing Lab. (n.d.). Retrieved Mar. 02, 2005, from Writing Lab Web site: http://www.mtlsd.org/Jefferson_Middle/writinglab.asp.

Kent, R. (1994). *The Mosquito Test*. Mt. Desert, ME: Windswept Publishers.

(———) (1997). *Room 109—The Promise of a Portfolio Classroom*. Portsmouth, NH: Heinemann—Boynton/Cook.

(———) (2000). *Beyond Room 109: Developing Independent Study Projects*. Portsmouth, NH: Heinemann—Boynton/Cook.

Kettle Moraine School District, (n.d.). Retrieved Mar. 07, 2005, from Kettle Moraine Writing Program Web site: http://district.kmsd.edu/~writing/writemain.htm.

"Key Points" *Because Writing Matters: Improving Student Writing in Our Schools*. (© 2005). Retrieved May 2, 2005, from http://www.writingproject.org/pressroom/writingmatters/keypoints.html

Kjesrud, R. (2005, Mar 01). On line/e mail tutoring vs face to face. Message posted to Writing Center Mailing List Digest, archived at http://www.ttu.edu/

Murphy, Christina and Steve Sherwood (Eds.). (2003). *The St. Martin's Sourcebook for Writing Tutors*, 2nd edition. New York: St. Martin's Press.

National Council of Teachers of English, (1989). The English Coalition Conference. Retrieved Mar. 28, 2005, from "Assumptions, Aims, and Recommendations of the Secondary Strand," Institutional Support Web site: http://www.ncte.org/about/over/positions/category/stand/107655.htm.

Rafoth, Ben. (2000). *A Tutor's Guide: Helping Writers One to One*. Portsmouth, NH: Heinemann.

Silva, P. (2004, October). Launching a high school writing center. *Praxis: A Writing Center Journal*, 2. Retrieved Jan 22, 2005, from http://uwc3.fac.utexas.edu:8000/%7Epraxis/Focus/focus_silva_f04.

Vygotsky, L.S. (1978). *Mind and Society: The Development of Higher Mental Processes*. Cambridge, MA: Harvard University Press.

White paper. (n.d.). Retrieved Feb. 05, 2005, from http://www.sharpened.net/glossary/definition.php?whitepaper.

Writing center. (n.d.). Retrieved Feb. 24, 2005, from http://www.branson.org/writingcenter.html.

Index